PRAISE FOR

Gossip

"[W]e may add gossip to the list of subjects that can be leaden in the hands of sociologists, professors, and other credentialed bores, but magic in the hands of a writer like Epstein, gifted in sifting the rich and amusing place our world is."

—*American Spectator*

"*Gossip* is a book that's every bit as alluring, cunning, complicated, and sometimes appalling as its subject." —*San Francisco Chronicle*

"[A]n engrossing little enquiry, part history and part cultural musing." —The Forward

"Well-researched . . . *Gossip* contains the things that have made [Epstein's] work so agreeable to so many readers: the acute insight, the apt observation, sound analysis, irony without angst, the playful treatment and humor, from gentle to laugh-out-loud, that can come at any moment." —*Washington Times*

"While Epstein's ruminations on how we became a nation of gawkers ring painfully true, it is his willingness to analyze delectable tidbits regarding authors, intellectuals, and other luminaries that enlivens the narrative. . . . Amusing and serious in equal measures, Epstein grants readers the pleasurable company of a master observer of humanity's foibles." —*Kirkus*, starred

"Delectable firsthand anecdotes and portraits . . . add to the pleasures of this serious appraisal. Readers who share Epstein's concern about gossip's power 'to invade privacy, to wreck lives' and his reluctance to wholly condemn it 'because I enjoy it too much' will find him disquieting and delightful." —*Publishers Weekly*

"A deliciously meandering history and keen analysis of gossip and its role in human affairs. . . . Epstein is in fine form." —*Booklist*

GOSSIP

THE UNTRIVIAL PURSUIT

Joseph Epstein

MARINER BOOKS
HOUGHTON MIFFLIN HARCOURT
BOSTON • NEW YORK

First Mariner Books edition 2012
Copyright © 2011 by Joseph Epstein

For information about permission to reproduce selections from this book,
write to Permissions, Houghton Mifflin Harcourt Publishing Company,
215 Park Avenue South, New York, New York 10003.

www.hmhbooks.com

Library of Congress Cataloging-in-Publication Data
Epstein, Joseph, date.
Gossip : the untrivial pursuit / Joseph Epstein.
p. cm.
Includes bibliographical references.
ISBN 978-0-618-72194-8   ISBN 978-0-547-84459-6 (pbk.)
1. Gossip. I. Title.
BJ1535.G6E67 2011
302.2'4—dc2   2010049804

Book design by Melissa Lotfy

Printed in the United States of America
DOC 10 9 8 7 6 5 4 3 2 1

The author is grateful for permission to quote from the following:
Historical Memoirs of the Duc de Saint-Simon, edited and translated by Lucy
Norton, reproduced by permission of the Estate of Lucy Norton.
Correspondence of Truman Capote: Copyright © 2004 by the
Truman Capote Literary Trust; reprinted by permission.

FOR SHARON ROSEN,

elegant cousin

Talk, Mr. Nathaniel Alden had discovered, was chiefly gossip, and gossip encouraged a morbid interest in matters that didn't concern one.

— GEORGE SANTAYANA, *The Last Puritan*

Mme de Saint-Simon, all goodness, tried in vain to check our more outrageous utterances, but the brakes were off, and there ensued the most fearful struggle between the expression of sentiments that, humanly speaking, were quite natural, and the sensation that they were not altogether Christian.

— *Memoirs of the Duc de Saint-Simon*

The two most interesting things in life are metaphysics and gossip.

— E. M. CIORAN

Contents

Part III: Private Become Public

Preface

This is a book about gossip, that much-excoriated yet apparently unstoppable human activity that knows neither historical nor cultural bounds. Educated fleas may not do it, but all human beings seem to enjoy that conspiratorial atmosphere of intimacy in which two or three people talk about another person who isn't in the room. Usually they say things about this person that he would prefer not to have said. They might talk about his misbehavior in any number of realms (sexual, financial, domestic, hygienic, or any other that allows for moral disapprobation) or about his frailties (his hypocrisy, tastelessness, immodesty, neuroses, etc.). Or they might just wish to analyze his character, attempting to get at why his has been a life of such extraordinary undeserved success or such unequivocally merited failure.

Gossip has of course long had a ferociously bad press. Trivial has its subject matter been deemed, vulgar and wayward its practitioners inevitably designated. The intellectual equivalent of chewing gum—such has been among the many unkind things it has been called. In the eighteenth century, the Duc de Saint-Simon, that busy courtier at the Versailles of Louis XIV, provides a brief portrait of the type of the gossip, about a jumped-up servant and social climber named Saumery, that reads with the bold caricatural quality of a Daumier drawing: "He put on airs and looked important, never perceiving that he was merely ill-bred. He whispered into people's ears or shielded his mouth with his hand, often sniggering, and then promptly disappearing, always filled with gossip." One needs to add here that the Duc de Saint-Simon's *Memoirs,* chronicling all that went on in the court of the Sun King, themselves provide one of the most sustained acts of high-grade gossip on historical record. But gossip, make no mistake, always implies a judgment.

Yet however bad the odor it has generally found itself in, gossip persists. More than persists, its power continues to grow, its sway to become more pervasive. Why, despite all the religious and secular strictures against it, does it refuse to go away? How has it come about that gossip has increased its domain extravagantly in recent decades, so that where once it was thought an activity best conducted over a backyard fence, usually believed to be engaged in by women, it now dominates the news and has become all but synonymous with leaks in high places that can help bring down governments, and has found vast reinvigoration on the Internet? Why is the appetite for gossip apparently unslakable? Why is it so enticing? What are its true functions? Who needs it? Why has it increased so in our own day?

These are but a few of the questions that are taken up in this book about an activity whose full meaning not all of us understand—including, as he sets out to investigate it, the author—but that most of us continue to enjoy.

The history of gossip has never been written—and it isn't, strictly speaking, written here—but if one were to sketch it out quickly, gossip would begin as an intimate and personal act most often carried on between two persons; then, with the advent of the printing press, it soon became public, with men and women earning their living discovering and purveying gossip to a mass audience, which of course continues in our day; the appetite for public gossip having been established, purveyors of it were never found to be in short supply, and in recent decades they have been immensely aided by the spread of cable television and the advent of the Internet. As the means, the technologies, of gossip have widened, so, naturally enough, has its influence.

If the reader of this book comes away with nothing else, I hope he will at least have realized that the major rap against gossip, that it is trivial, is no longer the main thing to be said about it, if ever it was. For gossip has come to play a larger and larger role in public life, and, as I argue, in ways that can thrum with significance and odd side effects.

I was drawn to the subject of gossip, first, because I took such pleasure in receiving it, having over the years had friends who were artful in conveying it, some of them working in fairly high places or living among putatively glamorous people. I am also drawn to the nature of gossip, which, though often false and not less often malicious, can also be a species of truth, deliverable in no other way than by word of mouth, personal letter, diaries and journals published posthumously, and not obtainable otherwise. Just because information is begun in gossip does not mean it can't also be true. Gossip's particular brand of truth is beguiling truth: beguiling in the sense of being enticing, charming, sometimes deceptive, and always in need of being strained through skeptical intelligence. Gossip can be mean, vicious even, yet also hugely entertaining, helpful, and important—and on occasion all of these things at once. The book you are about to read attempts to explain how and why this is.

I

PRIVATE GOSSIP

How It Works

Molly was a woman much on the telephone. When it
rang she had just enquired: "Well, what's the gossip?"

— DORIS LESSING, *The Golden Notebook*

CONSIDER GOSSIP IN its bare bones, the mechanics of
it, how it works. One person tells another person something about a third person that may or may not have a
basis in fact. Like as not, what the first person has to tell goes to
the absent person's reputation. Dealing with his personal life, it
usually serves to diminish or tarnish that reputation. Why did the
first person decide to tell it? Perhaps because he bears the absent
person a grudge. Perhaps because the absent person's behavior,
the subject of the item of gossip, angers or strongly puts him off.
Perhaps because he finds the behavior he is describing too amusing or freakish or astounding to withhold telling. Perhaps because
he is reasonably confident that he will be charming the person to
whom he is relaying the gossip, who will be indebted to him for
a few moments of entertainment. Perhaps because he senses that
conveying this bit of information will increase the intimacy between him and the person with whom he is gossiping.

Listening to gossip can be likened to receiving stolen goods; it
puts you in immediate collusion with the person conveying the
gossip to you. Sometimes the person who initiates the gossip asks

the person to whom he is telling it to keep it to himself. Sometimes secrecy is implied, sometimes not. If the gossip has an element of real excitement to it, the request that the item go no further is unlikely to be honored. Some of the best gossip is intramural, taking place within a smallish group: an office, a school, a neighborhood, a village or small town. My first encounter with gossip of this kind had to do with stories of sexual exploits that teenage boys at my high school told to other boys about the girls they went out with. "Kissing and telling" is the traditional term for this sort of gossip. There was during that time, to be sure, a fair amount of not kissing but telling anyway, or of obviously heightening and dramatizing one's rather pathetic conquests, a clear case of enhancing one's status by retailing false gossip.

In less intramural settings, often one's social perspective or one's politics will direct one's interest in gossip. Whether one thinks oneself liberal or conservative, one's field of gossip interest is likely to be very different. Conservatives were blown away by Bill Clinton stories, liberals made uneasy by them. Two persistent bits of gossip about Martin Luther King Jr. are that he amply plagiarized his doctoral thesis and that, though married, he had lots of love affairs, including a steady liaison with a woman who was a dean at Cornell. If one is an admirer of Dr. King's, one doesn't want to hear such stories; if one is not, or even if one is skeptical about public heroes generally, such gossip has its natural appeal in bringing down an ostensibly great man. An even better story has King determined to fire Jesse Jackson just before the end of his life—better, that is, for all those people who consider Jesse Jackson essentially a fraud. The same applies to John F. Kennedy stories; if you care for him, you are likely to be less attentive to all those upstairs-at-the-White-House stories with movie stars and Mafia molls, and if you don't much like him, bring on more such stories. Gossip, as the old *New York Post* gossip columnist Earl Wilson once put it, "is hearing something you like about someone you don't."

Not all gossip need be malicious, mean-spirited, vengeance-seeking, status-enhancing, though much of it is. All gossip starts out as people talking about other people. The distinction between gossip and rumors is that the latter are more often about incidents, events, supposed happenings, or things that are about to happen to people, and generally not about the current or past conduct of people; rumor tends to be unsubstantiated, events or incidents whose truth is still in the realm of speculation. Cass Sunstein, in his *On Rumors,* writes that rumors "refer roughly to claims of fact—about people, groups, events, and institutions—that have not been shown to be true, but that move from one person to another, and have credibility not because direct evidence is known to support them, but because other people seem to believe them." Compared to gossip, rumors are also less specific, more general, more diffuse, less personal in content and in the manner in which they are disseminated. Rumors can lead to gossip, and gossip can reinforce rumors. But gossip is particular, told to a carefully chosen audience, and is specifically information about other people.

Other people is the world's most fascinating subject. Apart from other people, there can only be shoptalk, or gab about sports, politics, clothes, food, books, music, or some similar general item. Talk is possible about the great issues and events and questions, both of the day and of eternity, about which most of us operate in the realm of mere opinion and often don't have all that much—or anything all that interesting—to say. How long, really, does one wish to talk, at least with friends, about the conditions for peace in the Middle East, the probable direction of the economy, the existence of God? For most of us, truth to tell, not very long.

So much easier, so much more entertaining, to talk about the decaying marriage of an acquaintance, the extravagant pretensions of in-laws, the sexual braggadocio of a bachelor friend. Most gossip, or most of the best gossip, is about dubious if not downright reprehensible behavior. The best of it is about people with whom one has a direct acquaintance. Served with a dash of humor it can be awfully fine stuff, even if one has never met the person being gossiped about.

Years ago a friend in London told me that the playwright Harold Pinter wrote rather poor poems—my friend called them, in fact, "pukey little poems"—that he sent out in multiple Xerox copies to friends, then sat back to await their praise. One such poem was about the cricketer Len Hutton, the English equivalent of Joe DiMaggio; the poem, in its entirety, runs: "I knew Len Hutton in his prime, / Another time, another time." After Pinter had sent out the copies, its recipients, as usual, wrote or telephoned to tell him how fine the poem was, how he had caught the matter with perfect laconic precision, how touched and moved they were by it—with the single exception of a man who made no response whatsoever. When Pinter hadn't heard from this man after two weeks, he called to ask if he had in fact received the poem. "Yes," said the man, "I have indeed." Unable to hold back, Pinter asked, "Well, Simon, what did you think of it?" Pausing briefly, the man replied, "Actually, I haven't quite finished it."

This is gossip on the model of a joke—gossip with a punch line. What is of greatest interest about it as an item of gossip is the continuing need on the part of its subject, a world-famous playwright, a Nobel Prize winner, for these driblets of praise. It is a story about pathetic vanity. One might think so successful a writer had already had more than his share of praise, but no scribbler seems ever to have had enough of what Thomas Mann called vitamin P. This is gossip as analysis, or test, of character, with the character, as in almost all good gossip in this realm, failing to pass.

I'm not sure that merely insulting someone behind his back, a variant of the catty remark, constitutes gossip. Another friend of mine not long ago wrote to me of an acquaintance of ours that his "appalling wife Janice made him the most famous cuckold in New York, but who can blame her?" I had known about my acquaintance's wife leaving him for another man, so this insult scarcely constituted news. Yet it is unclear whether the material of gossip always has to be new. Some gossip, of the species known as backbiting, can be about no more than two people re-hearsing the already well-known failings or sad tribulations of a third person.

"Well, I do a lot of talking and the 'I' is not often absent," the writer Elizabeth Hardwick told the man who interviewed her for the *Paris Review.* "In general I'd rather talk about other people. Gossip, or as we gossips like to say, character analysis." Isaac Rosenfeld, a writer who was one of the New York intellectuals of the 1940s and '50s, used jokingly to call such gossip "social analysis," and in this group the analysis was of a kind that took the skin off the person being gossiped about. The New York intellectuals brutally mocked one another's ambitions, sex practices, self-importance, and pretensions, all done behind the back, of course, and with much vicious inventiveness.

"Who is more devoid of human interest than those with nothing to hide?" asks a character in Frederic Raphael's recent novel *Fame and Fortune.* Some of us have grander things to hide than others; others may have very little to hide; but very few of us are free of being gossiped about, at least insofar as being criticized behind one's back constitutes gossip. Not long ago I was with a man who said that he had arrived at a point in life—he was soon to turn eighty—where he feared no gossip. True, he had no addictions, unless that of collecting books; had never cheated on his wife; was a good father; no scandal of any kind attached to him; he was modest in his pretensions—in all, led an honorable and quiet life. Yet, as I told him, he wouldn't in the least like it if I went about behind his back saying that his taste in food was atrocious (he prided himself on finding excellent, generally inexpensive ethnic restaurants), that his intellectual judgment was poor (he had enormous admiration for five or six writers, all social scientists except for Samuel Johnson), or that his opinions about music and movies were hopeless (he would not infrequently report on how much he enjoyed a concert or a new film). I can of course easily see people doing a similar job on me, attacking my writing, the way I dress, my own less than modest pretensions. If it were to get back to me that someone said that I was ungenerous, or coarse in my aesthetic judgments, or disloyal, it would sting, however low the truth quotient of the accusations. Nobody, the point being, is impregnable to gossip.

One definition of gossip is "bits of news about the personal affairs of others." These personal affairs are a man's or woman's stock of secrets; their ostensible secrecy is after all what makes them personal. Georg Simmel, that most brilliant of sociologists, claims that the secret is "one of the greatest achievements of humanity." By this I assume Simmel means that societies have erected rules, implicit and explicit, so that we are permitted freedom from intrusion on the part of others into our lives, and without this freedom to protect what we hold personal and most dear, all our lives would be a vast deal poorer. That which is most secret about us — our dreams, our hopes, our small vices, our fondest fantasies, however outrageous or unrealistic they may be — is often what is most significant to us. Intrusive gossip, given the chance, would make a sloppy meal of these, which is why it can be so damaging.

Not all gossip is engaged in for the purpose of hurting people. Gossip can be wildly entertaining. Sometimes analyzing the problems, flaws, and weaknesses of friends, even dear friends, sweeps one up and carries one away in sheer exuberance for the game. The philosopher Martin Heidegger, not everyone's idea of a whimsical fellow, thought gossip trivial and shallow and falsely authoritative, denying that it had much educational value. Yet I have been in gossip sessions where people delved into the motives of others in a manner that provided more in the way of knowledge than the highly opaque works of Herr Heidegger. Heidegger himself — notably his siding with the Nazis and then trying to cover it up, his love affair while married with his student Hannah Arendt — was the subject of some scorching, demoralizing, and highly entertaining gossip, and there was even more so after his death.

If ever there was a mixed bag, gossip provides it: it can be mean, ugly, vicious, but also witty, daring, entirely charming. It can be damning, dampening (of the spirits), dreary, but also exhilarating, entertaining, highly educational. It pops up in backwater villages among primitive tribes and in great cultural capitals. The only thing missing from the Garden of Eden was a third person for Adam and Eve to gossip about. Despite much railing against gossip, it doesn't look to be going away, not now, probably not ever.

Diary

Late on the dark afternoon of a cold day, I stepped into the Peet's coffee shop down the block from my apartment. Book in hand, I was expecting to read while sitting alone drinking my coffee. But then I saw S. L., the one person I taught with in the English department at Northwestern University for whom I retained a high regard. Still attractive, she had been twice divorced and had no children. She had a reputation for seriousness and for fearlessness; for academics, fearlessness meant saying precisely what one thought, a rare thing. She was said to be a no-nonsense teacher of whom students were at first terrified and then came to reverence. Although we were never close—never met alone for lunches or drinks, never really engaged in extended conversation—I hoped that she respected me as I did her.

She was by herself at a table near the window. She spotted me, and I waved from my place in line. When I was given my coffee, she signaled me to join her, which I did. I had retired from teaching four years earlier. She, though my contemporary, was, I gathered, still at it.

"Miss teaching at all?" she asked after I had taken off my coat and sat down across from her.

"Not a bit," I said. "I had a fairly decent run, but enough is enough. A teacher, as I suspect you've noticed, is a person who never says anything once."

"I have noticed," she replied with a slight sigh, "though

I prefer the definition of a teacher as someone who talks in other people's sleep. Auden said that, I think."

"The same cast of immensely attractive characters still at work in the English department?" I asked.

"Yep," she said, "the three D's, as I like to think of them: the depressed, the disappointed, and the deranged."

"Speaking of the latter, is it true that poor Ardis Lawrenson committed suicide?" I asked.

"Yep. She'd been an alcoholic for years, and they found her dead in her bathtub. Like Seneca, she had opened her veins."

"Jesus!"

"Yes, Jesus, mother, and Mary. I thought she was merely another secret academic drunk. I wouldn't have guessed she was wacky enough to take her life."

"Is Baumgartner still around?" Louis Baumgartner was one of the great figures in the department, a short man with muttonchops, a Renaissance English scholar whom a fatuous dean had been able to pry away from Stanford twenty or so years ago.

"Yes," she said. "Baumgartner and the missus, the Bummies, the dreary duo."

"Did you know that the students used to call Lily Baumgartner, with her considerable avoirdupois and her black bangs and her more than a hint of a mustache, 'Ollie,' after Oliver Hardy?"

"I never heard that one," she said. "The little bastards can be cruel, but here is a touch of creative cruelty I much admire."

"I suppose Baumgartner is by now too old to arrange for further offers from other universities, which he used to do to leverage up his own salary."

"No man—or woman either—is ever too old to be greedy and crummy," she said, "especially academic men and women. But did I ever tell you my story about Erich Heller and the Baumgartners?" Erich Heller was a Czech literary critic, Jewish and gay, of deep Teutonic culture, who taught in the German department and until his death was one of the most distinguished people at the university.

"No, never. I liked Erich a lot. Toward the end of his life, I used to go to lunch with him every three weeks or so. Even his snobbery — he used to talk about his good friend Isaiah Berlin a bit too much and with too great reverence for my taste — didn't bother me. But tell me about Erich and the Baumgartners."

"We were at lunch together not long after the Baumgartners arrived at Northwestern. Erich leaned over and asked me if I knew the Baumgartners, which in his thick accent came out sounding like 'the Bum's Gardeners.' I said yes, that I had met them a time or two.

"'Last night I was with them at Rudy's [the dean of the arts college at the time],' Erich said, giving the *R* a pretty good workout, 'and I was seated next to this Mrs. Bum's Gardener. An excruciatingly boring woman, let me assure you. What a creature! I am not an unimaginative man, but try though I might, I couldn't imagine making love to such a woman. I couldn't imagine it, I tell you, I just couldn't.' His voice grew shrill. He seemed terrified at the prospect of being thrown in bed with Lily Baumgartner. I patted his hand. 'Don't worry, Erich,' I said to him. 'No one is ever going to ask you to do so.'"

"The story suggests to me," I said, "that perhaps Baumgartner deserved all those raises for nothing more than sleeping with Mrs. Baumgartner all these years."

We went on to talk about the other people in the department. S. L. knew where all the bodies were buried. She anatomized the extravagant vanity of the poets — turning out, as she said, "their hopeless little dribblings." I mentioned the poet who regularly sent out e-mails announcing he had won some new negligible prize.

"God, yes," she said. "All his dubious achievements must be made known. I keep waiting for him to send a university-wide e-mail announcing that he had an excellent bowel movement over the previous weekend."

She went on to puncture the exaggerated pretensions of the "so-called" (her qualification) scholars in the department. She knew who had attempted suicide, who was living with a lesbian partner, who had a secret drinking problem, who spoke against a putative friend at a closed meeting who was up for tenure, who attained to new heights of pomposity and unreality in his or her behavior. I added my own, on the whole less rich, bits to this splendid stew of gossip.

We were at this game for perhaps an hour and a half. S. L. served up her items with a fine rinse of cold irony. I laughed as I listened to her take the air out of many of my former colleagues' pretensions. (Had she ever, I couldn't help for a fearful moment wondering, turned in a similar demolition job on me?) Over ninety or so minutes not a positive word was uttered, no attempt at fair assessment ventured; it was purely slash and burn, with lots of salt poured on wounds.

I couldn't remember when I had had such a delightful time.

2

Feasible, Uncheckable, Deeply Damning

If people really knew what others said about them,
there would not be two friends left in the world.

— BLAISE PASCAL

T HE MOST ARRESTING news, at least as journalists
tend to look at the matter these days, is what someone
doesn't want known. Hence all the current interest in
investigative journalism, which is a dignified phrase for the activity of muckraking, whose goal is exposé. Gossip is very close
to, and all but perfectly congruent with, this conception of the
news: it, too, is almost always about what someone doesn't want
known. In its baldest sense, gossip is revealing the secrets of others, though, as we shall see, it is not that alone.

In recent years, sociologists have been widening the definition of the word "gossip," so that it includes the useful passing on
of information as well as the older meaning of casual or uncon-
strained talk about other people, often with at least slightly malicious intent and not necessarily confirmed as true. The latter is of
course the traditional gossip that the Bible and the Talmud and
every small-town minister inveigh against, generally to negligible
effect.

Just as the institution and industry of prostitution took a powerful hit from the easing up of sexual restraints among ordinary women, so has gossip taken a hit from our therapeutic age, which has encouraged the act of easy confession among friends and even acquaintances. If I voluntarily inform you of my own weaknesses and mistakes — my weird sexual habits, my addictions, my deceptions, my vicious acts, my serious and petty vices — it deprives you of the opportunity of hearing it in the intimate, conspiratorial atmosphere of gossip from someone else. Gossip is at its height when it carries a touch of exposé, revealing things not hitherto known, preferably with at least a hint of scandal added. Oscar Wilde remarked that "scandal is gossip made tedious by morality," an odd thing to say for a man whose own life was destroyed by gossip turned into scandal, with nothing tedious about it.

The best gossip also has a private, an exclusive, feeling about it. "You mustn't tell anyone about this, but . . ." or "Just between us . . ." or "This must go no farther . . ." are phrases that, for people who enjoy gossip, carry the equivalent magic of the fairy-tale opening of "Once upon a time." The most enticing gossip is that which is highly feasible, often uncheckable, and deeply damning of the person who is its subject. Should the "item," as Walter Winchell, in his day the world's most famous and powerful gossip columnist, used to call his stories, also turn out to be true, so much the better. The so-called blind item, begun by Winchell, is still in use in our day. Here, from the August 28, 2009, Page Six of the *New York Post,* is a small gathering of such items:

> WHICH well-liked pro golfer once switched sponsors because he needed several million dollars in hush money? Seems he knocked up a stripper while playing at the Firestone Country Club in Akron, Ohio, and had to pay her off to keep their love child a secret . . . WHICH cable news anchor should be more careful with his cellphone? After he recently misplaced it, a coworker opened it up and found a nude photo of the anchor's girlfriend . . . WHICH political leader in the Caribbean is under investigation by the US government for using foreign aid to ren-

ovate his palatial home? The $443,000 spent was falsely listed as "security and road improvements."

Another problem for gossip tossed up by the modern age is sometimes to decide what behavior is damning, let alone deeply so. Given high divorce rates, is marital infidelity, for example, still worthy of gossip? Perhaps so, but even though it is still an act of betrayal, at least if carried on by only one party to the marriage, it no longer has quite the same moral repugnance it once did. People might still be appalled but surely no longer shocked by it. Or nowadays, with people regularly coming out to admit their suppressed homosexuality, is someone who has an undercover homosexual life worth gossiping about? Perhaps, but again, the frisson seems somehow lower than once it might have been. Or what about revealing a person's wealth, or the way he or she came by it? Balzac says that behind every great fortune is a crime; good gossip would speculate on the precise nature of that crime, but in this realm, too, we are perhaps less easily shocked than at any earlier time.

From the standpoint of gossip, there is still something entertaining about a politician notable for his strong stand on family values being caught in the company of a young man or boy with whom he is having what H. L. Mencken used to call "non-Euclidian sex." When Senator Larry Craig, a Republican of Idaho, one such family-values politician, was caught in acts of (homosexual) misconduct in a Minneapolis–St. Paul airport restroom in 2007, people were less shocked, I suspect, than amused to have another hypocrite uncovered. William Bennett, the former secretary of education, writes books on virtue and is revealed to have lost three million dollars on slot machines in Las Vegas. The serious gamblers I know were not shocked but amazed that he would be so foolish as to lose the money playing slots, which notoriously favor the house. These days, it seems, one has only to come out for family values or virtue and scandal is certain to follow.

Here is a bit of gossip I heard not long ago that I think qualifies as gossip-worthy, even in a nearly shockproof culture, and that deserves diagnosis precisely for its shock value. The names must be suppressed in print, as they probably wouldn't be if I were telling this story to you in person, because of fear of libel. (Much gossip is slanderous, the distinction between libel and slander being that the former is usually presented in print or in a movie or some other public version, the latter in speech or conversation.) Someone not long ago told me that a famous American writer had committed incest with her son. I asked the person who told me this whence he came into this notable piece of information, and he said that he heard it from a woman he knows who went to college with the writer's son, and that the son had revealed it to her in a fit of depression.

Incest—surely it still rings the gong of striking gossip. Outside redneck jokes, incest, I confess, gets my attention. The story nicely meets the criteria of the plausible, the uncheckable, and the deeply damning. *Plausible:* The woman about whom this story was told was sexually adventurous, which makes her seem a likely participant in incest. *Uncheckable:* Journalistic criteria of reliable sources would not work here. To go to the woman to whom the son is supposed to have confessed this story of incest with his mother wouldn't be good enough. He could, after all, have been lying to her, if only to make himself seem more exotic. The woman, too, for reasons we don't know, could be lying; she may have a motive that is unavailable to us for spreading such a story. One could go to the son and simply ask him, Did your mother invite you into her bed for sex, and did you take her up on the invitation? He could deny it, either truthfully or by lying. He could also choose to punch one in the nose. The mother could confirm it, but she happens to be dead. *Deeply damning:* So it strikes me, and so I suspect incest strikes most others, too, though I am sure there are lots of people in an unhinged culture ready to say, à la the characters on *Seinfeld,* "Not that there's anything wrong with it."

Gossiping can be a dangerous activity. In 1976, the comedienne Carol Burnett sued the *National Enquirer* for reporting her "boisterous" (a tabloid code word for drunk) behavior in a Manhattan restaurant and acting disruptively around Henry Kissinger and his guests who were dining at the same restaurant. Carol Burnett sued and, after an extended legal battle, won. More recently, in Hooksett, New Hampshire, in the town's building department, office workers began a story about their boss having an affair with an office secretary. The story evidently wasn't true, and the four women most prominent in spreading it were fired by the town council. The women have since sued the Town of Hooksett to get their jobs back.

Many years ago I was in the office at City University of New York of the literary critic Irving Howe. On his desk was a copy of the thick manuscript of a book that he was to call *World of Our Fathers,* which was to bring him considerable commercial success. Howe's reputation in the world of intellectual journalism was at its height, and yet he seemed melancholy. "I sometimes ask myself why bother," he said to me. "What's all this endless work really about?" Then he leaned in and said, "You know, someone not long ago told me that L. C. [I have chosen not to furnish her real name or initials] remarked to her, 'Irving Howe, just another Jewboy in a hurry.'" Now the real gossip content in this story is that L. C., a notably liberal woman, would make so blatantly anti-Semitic a remark. The story isn't about Irving Howe at all, but about L. C. Irving Howe and L. C. are now both dead, and yet, if I spelled out her full name, her reputation would be marred by this shameful remark. At the same time, by not giving her name, I drain this story of much of its value as good gossip.

A story I found in a gossip-rich book called *The Grand Surprise: The Journals of Leo Lerman* will give some sense of what naming people can add to the bite of gossip. In his journal entry for January 6, 1969, Lerman, a man who seemed to have known every celebrity in journalism and the arts in Manhattan and who was for most of his career a writer and editor for Condé Nast magazines, writes: "Onassis likes to fuck women up their asses. Mrs. Kennedy won't do it." Maria Callas—the original source of the story, an earlier lover of Onassis's, and a friend of Lerman's—told some friends that "being fucked up the ass hurt and was boring." This is going perhaps further than most people would prefer to go: gossip about not merely sexual preferences but the gory details of those preferences. Yet its ghastly privateness—that and the celebrity status of the names: Kennedy, Callas, Onassis—qualifies it for what one might call powerful low-grade high-level gossip, or would that be high-grade low-level gossip?

I have an English friend who dines at higher tables than I, who many years ago asked if I could guess with whom Fidel Castro was currently sleeping. Given the wide field of possibilities, I replied that I hadn't a clue. He encouraged me to try. I put forth the names of Indira Gandhi, Dyan Cannon, and Lee Radziwill. Wrong, not even close, are you kidding? were his responses. The answer turned out to be Kathleen Tynan, the wife of the drama critic Kenneth Tynan. Here was this beautiful literary adventuress in the bed of the world's last successful (successful for him; not, unfortunately, successful for his country) revolutionary. Was it true? Plausible it certainly was. The Tynans were very left wing in their sympathies, and Castro would have seemed a great man to them. I made a mental note to ask Fidel about the authenticity of the story the next time I encountered him. Alas, the meeting has yet to come about. I also neglected to ask my friend how he came to know this. Still, the story bears repeating, at least in a book about gossip.

Gossip about people one doesn't know, or was never in close contention of knowing, crops up with some frequency, and not only at the Fidel Castro level. Lots of it is available in published diaries, memoirs, and collections of letters. T. S. Eliot, that most discreet of writers, as a young man wrote to his friend Conrad Aiken that "letters should be indiscretions—otherwise they are simply official bulletins." Autobiography is a form in which one gets to gossip about oneself—often, let me add, with roughly the same degree of truthfulness as gossip generally—and today people do so more and more, specializing in writing about their shortcomings. Why, for an unpleasant example, did Laurence Olivier in his autobiography need to tell us that his premature ejaculations complicated his marriage to Vivien Leigh? Who set the gossip going that Olivier and Danny Kaye were homosexual lovers?

Some gossip about the famous makes its way down the historical grapevine, taking years to arrive. I only recently heard that the dull and dreary Duke of Windsor, in an item of this kind, is supposed to have said that Mrs. Wallis Simpson, the woman for whom he gave up the British crown, was the best fellatrix in Europe; Tennessee Williams claims this in his memoirs. A perfect piece of historical gossip, wonderfully uncheckable, but it also has to be set alongside rivaling gossip that has the Duke of Windsor a not-so-secret homosexual, though one bit of gossip doesn't necessarily eliminate the other. I have myself long been in favor of the notion that the rather androgynous Mrs. Simpson was actually a man, a speculation that, if true, could make both stories work together beautifully.

The gossip about the former British press lord Conrad Black and his wife, Barbara Black, who had been much in the press during the time of the legal charges against Lord Black that he stole money from the shareholders of the media company he began, had to do with his social pretensions and his wife's extravagance. In *The New Yorker*, a former friend is cited remarking that it is a good thing that Conrad has been able to wheedle himself into the House of Lords because it gave him a chance, as the son of a rich man, for the first time in his life to meet some ordinary people. In *Vanity Fair* another anonymous person is quoted as saying that perhaps five or six women in the world are able to dress as expensively as Barbara Black, and she is not one of them. These are both examples of the catty remark as a branch of gossip, and a reminder that malice dipped lightly in wit helps to enliven gossip and send it on its mischievous way.

Here is an item that might come under the category of The Way We Live Now: Someone told me—or did I read it somewhere?—that the sperm used to conceive the photographer Annie Leibovitz's child came from the son of her partner, Susan Sontag (though Ms. Leibovitz maintains that the sperm came from a sperm bank). If true, would this have made Sontag, had she lived, simultaneously the co-mother and grandmother of this child? Again, if true, this may well be something that the parties mentioned would prefer not to have known. Or have contemporary lives, at least those of the moderately celebrated, become so deprivatized, not to say depraved, that the spread of such information wouldn't be in the least troublesome to any of them?

Allow me to pause here to say that I do not feel altogether comfortable purveying all this gossip, much of it acquired at third or fourth hand. I tell myself I am doing it to demonstrate some of the more exotic forms gossip in our day can take. I am using it, too, I suppose, in the hope of drawing you further into this book with the promise of more, even juicer items. My discomfort derives from the fact that there is still a thing called good taste, and I am reasonably sure that I have already outraged it several pages ago.

Someone writing a book on gossip — or on any subject for that matter — ought to be as clear as he can about his fundamental attitude to the subject. Does he find gossip amusing or largely pernicious, entertaining or chiefly in bad taste? Or does he hold all these words to be meaningless in connection with gossip, because he finds it another of those aspects of human nature about which we simultaneously ought not to be excessively proud and yet understand that there isn't the least hope for reform?

I cannot condemn gossip, at any rate not with a good conscience, if only because I enjoy it too heartily, even while I understand that too much of it lowers the tone of any society (later I shall take up the question of whether this has actually happened) in which it takes place, not to say often ruins reputations and destroys lives. Yet all my life I have delighted in hearing delicious gossip, and I have also felt the strange but genuine pleasure of passing it along and, on occasion, purveying original gossip. Are these guilty pleasures, or pleasures that require no apology? Isaiah Berlin, the Oxford don famous for his social fluency, in a letter to Marion Frankfurter, the wife of the Supreme Court justice, wrote: "I can never actually stop myself from saying what I want to say either about or to people — if I do life immediately loses all possible savour and I see no point in carrying on at all." Shameless, perfectly shameless, yet I do believe I know whereof Sir Isaiah spoke, and perhaps you do, too.

Diary

Dinner in Washington that night in 1991 was supposed to be a foursome: Irving and Bea Kristol (who is also Gertrude Himmelfarb, the historian of Victorian intellectual life), the painter Helen Frankenthaler, and I. The Kristols had been living in Washington for some while; Helen and I were in town for a meeting of the National Council of the National Endowment for the Arts, of which we were at the time both members. Dinner was scheduled for 7 p.m. in the dining room of the Four Seasons Hotel.

At 5 p.m. Bea called to ask if it would be all right if Dick and Lynne Cheney joined us after dinner for coffee and dessert. I said of course, it was fine with me. Dick Cheney was then the secretary of defense and successfully conducting the Persian Gulf War against Iraq and not yet the great ogre that his political adversaries enjoy making of him; Lynne was then chair of the National Endowment for the Humanities. Lynne, Bea Kristol said, would appreciate the opportunity to talk to Helen and me about how things were run at the Endowment for the Arts.

The Cheneys arrived a bit after eight. The Secret Service men with their walkie-talkies accompanying them waited out in the foyer of the restaurant. Dick and Lynne Cheney had come from a movie, shown especially for them at the American Film Institute, for the kind of fame that Dick Cheney had at that moment did not allow him to take his wife to an ordinary movie theater. I remember how self-effacing, how modest, Dick Cheney seemed that night. At one point a congressman with a Mittel European accent, Tom Lantos by name, came up to the table to shake his hand and tell him how well he was running the Gulf War. At another point, our waiter arrived to say that someone in the room wished to buy champagne for our table in honor of Dick Cheney's efforts, but Cheney refused, quietly asking the waiter to thank the man who had made the offer.

Much of the talk over coffee and dessert was among Lynne Cheney, Helen Frankenthaler, and me. She asked us a number of questions about the NEA, which we answered as best we could. Her husband didn't seem to mind her dominating the talk at table. Perhaps it was a relief to be silent after crowded days at the Pentagon and after appearing so frequently on television, which he did, almost hourly it seemed, with Colin Powell at his side, to answer questions on how the war was going.

After ninety minutes or so, the Cheneys left the restaurant. I found myself much impressed by them. So, too, did Helen Frankenthaler, who said: "She is a very bright woman. Her questions were genuinely penetrating. Very impressive. Really smart, Lynne Cheney. But tell me, her husband, what does he do?"

Bea, Irving, and I looked at one another.

"Actually," I said, "he's secretary of defense."

I don't recall Helen's response. I do recall the graciousness of the Kristols at not lingering over this, and that the rest of our evening together went along just fine.

3

When Is It All Right to Gossip?

Don't speak well of your friend, for although you will start
with his good traits, the discussion might turn to his bad traits.

— THE TALMUD

IF GOSSIP IS telling things about other people that they
would rather not have known, then gossip also means, in
plainer words, breaching secrets. Benjamin Franklin said,
"Three may keep a secret if two are dead." Most people feel that
they can keep secrets; probably few really can. Because of this,
gossip, I think we may be assured, will never go out of business.

"Hardly any men but born gentlemen or men of culture are
capable of keeping a secret," wrote La Bruyère, though some of
the most cultured people I know have the largest appetites for
gossip of the secret-breaking kind. In an earlier age, a lady or a
gentleman was not supposed to engage in the purveying of secrets in the form of gossip, either telling it or receiving it; good
taste argued against doing so. Gossip was another word for idle
or loose talk, and was thought to be petty and mean. It was—in-
correctly—viewed as an act engaged in chiefly by women who
had nothing better to do with their time. Most people who have
looked into the matter conclude that men gossip just as much as
women, with the same frequency, intensity, and relish.

The gossip spectrum runs from acts of disloyalty at a maximum to those of mild indiscretion at a minimum. (*Discreet Indiscretions* is the title of a useful monograph on gossip by the German sociologist Jörg Bergmann.) The disloyalty fades and the indiscretion lessens the further the remove of the gossiper from the actual parties being gossiped about. Someone recently told me, for example, that a gynecologist told him that when his patient Elizabeth Taylor came in for a minor surgical procedure she brought along security men to make sure that all her pubic hair, some of which needed to be shaved, would be swept up and properly disposed of, lest any of the nurses or orderlies on the job attempted to scoop it up and offer it for sale on eBay. This story feels mightily like gossip, yet I do not feel the least disloyalty in passing it along; instead I feel myself merely lapsing into wretched bad taste in retelling it. I also feel that, in the current age, it is probably a true story.

Gossip is, of course, a form of news. A character in *Scoop*, Evelyn Waugh's novel about journalism, says of the news that it is what people want to read, except once it's printed it's no longer news and hence not of much interest. The less widespread, the less well known, the news, the more potent, by virtue of its exclusivity, and the more interesting it is. Serious gossip ought to be an intimate affair, one person telling another, two or three others at most, something hitherto unknown about an absent person. Too widely broadcast, gossip, like the news once printed, no longer holds much interest. (Not that this stops the tabloid press from running the same stories—about Oprah's weight loss and gain, Brad Pitt's boredom in marriage, and the rest—over and over again. Enquiring minds, it seems, can take lots of tedious repetition.) And like the news itself, gossip is generally of interest only if it is bad news.

"No one," Bertrand Russell remarked, "gossips about other people's secret virtues." Although rare, gossip about goodness is, theoretically, possible. Revealing the name of a large anonymous donor to an unequivocally excellent charity would be an example of such gossip. Other, smaller acts of generosity and kindness, which would seem bragging if told by the person who committed these acts, are best recounted as gossip: A tells B about an act of extraordinary selflessness on the part of C, who is much too modest to tell it herself. Gossip of this sort, the reverse of mischievous, is doing, one might say, the Lord's work in reminding people that there is much unmotivated goodness in the world. Yet even in these instances it is in the nature of gossip to find behind the most altruistic acts low motives — expiating guilt, moral exhibitionism, tax write-offs. Perhaps here the Talmudic injunction that provides the epigraph for this chapter comes into play: saying nice things about people can lead, in the natural rhythms of intimate conversation, to negative gossip.

Sociologists have for some while been at work on a rescue operation on gossip, attempting to uncover and point up its various social uses. In certain settings — the workplace, in large corporate offices, in government, in universities — gossip, as a source of funneling rumors recounting what is happening in the inner sanctum of an institution, may be the only way that workers have of finding out beforehand decisions that might have momentous effects on their future. Gossip can also be a relatively efficient way in which to acquire knowledge of the character of colleagues. Surely it would be invaluable to know that the woman with whom one is in competition for an important corporate vice presidency is sleeping with the CEO.

Universities are unimaginable without gossip, about who is to be promoted, whose ambitions have been denied, who is making what salary, who secretly loathes whom, or what new positions are about to be on offer, not to mention who is bedding down with whom. Being in on such gossip can be crucial to a successful academic career.

I recently went to dinner with good neighbors in the condominium building in which I live, where I learned, via what I suppose must be called gossip, the following: that another neighbor hadn't died exercising on his bicycle, as I'd thought, but by having an artery nicked during an angiogram; that a new couple who had recently moved in were in fact married, despite the woman's using a different last name than her husband; that another neighbor, a bachelor in his early sixties who had recently moved out of the building, was happily resettled in his new neighborhood and that lots of women in the building where he now lived were in mild pursuit of him; that a disagreeable neighbor was in a losing rivalry with a brother who had done much better in the world than he, which may be behind his general aggressiveness; that the janitor of the building is, after twenty-five years of marriage, going through a divorce; that another neighbor, after a stomach-reduction surgery, had had to go back into the hospital for a number of corrective surgeries.

My neighbor was reporting things that the people who had undergone them were unlikely to report to me, perhaps because they, mistakenly, take me to be uninterested in such information. Quite as likely, I am less successfully inquisitive than the neighbor, a bright and lively woman, who filled me in on these useful items. All this is gossip without the edge of malice; it is gossip as useful information, and I was pleased to be in possession of it.

As such, it is a confirming instance of the notion of sociologists and anthropologists that being let in on gossip not only gives people a surer sense of what is going on but allows them to feel better integrated in the life around them. Social scientists in recent years have begun to find the role of gossip in groups a research-worthy subject. According to David Sloan Wilson, a professor of biology and anthropology at Binghamton University, "gossip appears to be a very sophisticated, multifunctional interaction which is important in policing behavior in a group and defining group membership." If one is having trouble with a boss or co-worker, this argument runs, it helps to learn that other people are having similar difficulties—it makes one feel less odd, less alone. Sarah R. Wert, a psychologist at the University of Colorado adds: "We all know people who are not calibrated to the social world at all, who if they participated in gossip sessions would learn a whole lot of stuff they need to know and can't learn anywhere else, like how reliable people are, how trustworthy. Not participating in gossip at some level can be unhealthy, and abnormal." Yet in a paper called "A Social Comparison Account of Gossip," in the *Review of General Psychology,* Professor Wert and her colleague Peter Salovey allow that "gossip is overlooked by psychologists, both as an interesting phenomenon itself and as a promising venue for studying social comparison, stereotyping, in-group/out-group processes, attributional processes, and many other psychological phenomena."

Most people in corporate, governmental, and academic institutions have no other way of finding things out besides through gossip. Rumors stimulate gossip, of course: the company's headquarters are being moved to Phoenix and the CEO isn't going to make the move. Gossip of this kind doesn't usually violate anyone's rights; it isn't purveyed maliciously. Doubtless there is a good deal else that qualifies as useful and harmless gossip—gossip, that is, which doesn't betray other people's personal secrets or doesn't diminish or disparage them, even if conveyed behind their backs. Yet it goes to the heart of the matter to ask why good or useful gossip is, in the minds of most people, not what gossip is really about.

Lots of gossip floats in the ether of the morally gray. Consider the possibility that a good friend has the beginnings of serious depression, or worse, is entering into dementia. Ought one to discuss this behind his back with other of this friend's friends? And even if one has his best interests at heart, isn't one nevertheless gossiping—telling things he would hate having told about himself behind his back? And yet not to do so is to render his friends sadly, if not dangerously, ignorant of a matter about which they at least need to be informed. Not to talk—not to gossip, really—about this is to withhold significant information.

Gossip can also be useful for checking one's own status. In 1944 C. S. Lewis delivered a lecture to undergraduates at the University of London called "The Inner Ring." In this lecture Lewis argues that most of us imagine cliques or groups to which we yearn to belong; from the outside we see these inner circles as immensely appealing, and are ready to go to great lengths to be admitted to them:

> I don't believe that the economic motive and the erotic motive account for everything that goes on in what we moralists call the World. Even if you add Ambition I think the picture is still incomplete. The lust for the esoteric, the longing to be inside, takes many forms which are not easily recognizable as Ambition. We hope, no doubt, for tangible profits from every Inner Ring we penetrate: power, money, liberty to break rules, avoidance of routine duties, evasion of discipline. But all these would not satisfy us if we did not get in addition the delicious sense of secret intimacy . . . But we don't value the intimacy only for the sake of convenience; quite equally we value the convenience as a proof of the intimacy.

Lewis's point about our seeking acceptance in Inner Rings makes one wonder if one hasn't oneself, out of a weak yearning for social acceptance, told other people gossip, possibly damning gossip, for no other reason than the desire for their approval. Providing gossip is after all one of the ways that may help a person get into an Inner Ring of one's yearning. Having people inside the Ring share gossip with one may also signify that one has at last arrived as a member in good standing of the Inner Ring. Of course, as Lewis underscores, it is better not to be so insecure, so weak, as to be worried about being accepted by the right people in the first place, but alas, most of us are.

The most delicious gossip penetrates privacy; the assumption behind all gossip is that secret behavior is being uncovered. When it spreads in a way that gets out of control, gossip can result in the loss of income for the person gossiped about, the destruction of a marriage or an important friendship, public humiliation, jail, even suicide. Gossip can be dangerous.

Yet why is hidden bad behavior more pleasing to contemplate in the realm of gossip than modest good behavior? People tend to act badly not always because they are intrinsically bad but often because they are weak or in some way deficient. Bad behavior of this kind sounds like the adult version of categories that used to appear on the right-hand, or deportment, side of old grammar school report cards: does not work well with others, untidy, poor work habits. In the report card of adult gossip the categories have been changed: sleeps with women other than his wife, does drugs or is a secret boozer, is hooked on cosmetic surgery, business failing owing to extravagance, surreptitiously suppresses (or releases) his true sexual orientation.

Being gossiped about is one of the potential penalties one pays for bad, or sometimes merely unorthodox, behavior. If one does things that are unethical, devious, or mean, if one acts in ways that go against the grain of one's own pretensions to decent behavior, or through one's behavior attacks the reigning values of one's time, then, if caught out at any of these things, one shouldn't be surprised to find oneself the subject of gossip. The notorious and the infamous are always prime subjects for gossip; it is, in fact, one of gossip's main tasks to turn people notorious and infamous.

Gossip about people judged to be acting badly can also be gossip that, as the social scientists have it, enforces a community's norms. Although this is rarely its motive, gossip can act as a potential barrier to bad behavior, and in this sense can be a useful deterrent to such behavior. Some people will be restrained from acting badly if only because they fear that their conduct will be talked about behind their backs. Everything here depends, of course, on the quality of the community's norms. If these norms are far from admirable, gossip of this kind turns naturally ugly. Illustrations of the effects of this kind of gossip are available in Nathaniel Hawthorne's *The Scarlet Letter* and, much later, in Sinclair Lewis's novels *Babbitt* and *Main Street,* where conformity to a community's norms is crucial to one's adjustment to adult life, though often, as both Hawthorne and Lewis make clear, at the exorbitant price of the loss of one's true spirit and authentic personality.

Gossip can work the other way around, and loosen a community's norms, in a positive sense, by increasing tolerance. Reading about the behavior of the famous in gossip columns, people begin to think that their behavior, though it goes beyond established boundaries, perhaps isn't so terrible after all. In the 1970s and '80s, for example, famous athletes and movie stars—Muhammad Ali, Woody Allen, and others—began to have children out of wedlock. Whether one thinks this a good or a bad idea—I myself don't think it is such a hot idea—the fact is that by the public knowledge of the famous having had such children, birth out of wedlock among the unfamous became, for better and worse, gradually less disgraceful.

In his essay "The Ethics of Gossiping," the philosopher Emrys Westacott writes: "I do not believe there is a single general principle that by itself enables us to distinguish between permissible and impermissible talk about others." Context for the gossip can be—usually is—crucial. Perhaps even more crucial is motive. What did the person who set the gossip loose in the world have in mind? Here are only a few of the many possibilities:

The first, and most miserable, is that he wants to do dirt to the person he is gossiping about; he wants his reputation besmirched. He dislikes him, is envious of him, or feels that he has somewhere along the line made his life worse and finds gossip a splendid weapon of revenge. He is therefore quite willing to stretch the truth, even to lie, through the medium of gossip. Propelled by malice, such gossip is obviously ethically unacceptable, which doesn't mean that it hasn't always existed, or figures soon to desist.

Another, less direct motive for gossip is sheer jolly prurience. Here the item one hears about is simply too juicy not to pass along. Usually, though not always, such items are about sex: someone is secretly gay, or having affairs with a mother and her daughter simultaneously, or was caught by a husband *in flagrante,* or is contemplating a sex-change operation. One gossips about such things because one feels fairly confident that they will capture people's attention, will bring pleasure through titillation. Most of us have a taste for hearing about things we ourselves dare not do. Being seduced into listening to such items of gossip is the conversational equivalent of luscious-looking but, one discovers upon eating them, slightly waxy chocolates. One probably should refrain, but . . . oh, what the hell.

A third motive for gossip is the purely informational, though the context may be highly personal. A friend is contemplating a divorce, or on the verge of losing his business, or has become so depressed that she has resorted to electroconvulsive therapy. Here, without malice aforethought, the view is that key people ought to know about such matters.

A fourth motive for gossip may be the simple appetite for analysis of other men and women, friends included. Two friends begin talking about a third friend whom both like. What a good person she is, they both agree. No question, yet isn't it odd that at her age she seems unable to break away from her parents? And why, in her three marriages, has she never had children of her own? People said to have had unhappy childhoods are themselves less likely to want to bring children into the world to suffer as they did as kids. Do you suppose that is the reason she never had children? Or is she perhaps unable to reproduce for some physiological reason? And if so, which one? Well, you see where a taste for pure analysis, even of good friends, can lead. Directly, it turns out, to where the Talmudic quotation at the beginning of this chapter suggests it might.

But the motives for passing along gossip are perhaps beyond counting. The next time you find yourself setting an item of gossip in play, or just passing along such an item, you might do well to ask why you are doing so. What have you gained—or at least think you have gained—from your gossiping? What, in other words, is in it for you? As a man who gossips as much as most people, I have begun to ask myself this question, sometimes with interesting, sometimes with somewhat sadly degrading, results, none of which, be assured, has come near causing me to stop.

Diary

In the late 1960s, when racial integration was still thought an issue—and not yet largely viewed as a just aspiration, even in large northern American cities—the word got back to me, through the wife of a local minister, that gossip was going around in the all-white neighborhood I was then living in that I was looking for a Negro (as the word then was) buyer for the house I had put on the market. The neighborhood was working class. I, a Jew who had helped to organize a town meeting on integration, was thought to be very left wing. Rumor and gossip rode nicely in tandem here; it all made sense. Why wouldn't I look for a black family to sell my house to? Except that the story was entirely groundless. I was looking for any buyer I could find.

Here was a case of gossip having the reverse effect of reinforcing the community's norms. Learning about this gossip made me, in fact, hope for a black buyer, and left me more than a touch disappointed that none ever showed up to make an offer.

4

In the Know

He [John F. Kennedy] adored gossip, and I could tell him
what was going on around town. You must understand
that—that was one reason he liked you.

— BEN BRADLEE

T O BE A person on whom nothing is lost is the ideal established by Henry James in his exquisitely subtle novels.
Gossip is a strong element in many of these novels, and
the weighing and final assessment of the gossip, along with an ex-
amination of the motives behind it, is usually crucial to their de-
nouements. But many people who have never read Henry James,
or perhaps have never heard of him, wish to approximate, as best
they can, his ideal of being a person on whom nothing is lost.
They indulge in gossip in the hope that nothing significant or salacious or amusing or outrageous is going on in their worlds, or in
worlds beyond their own, without their knowing about it.

To be out of it, in the dark, clueless, this is a condition to which
no one but a saint, and maybe not even a saint, would aspire. To
be in the know, up on the real lowdown, in the loop, in possession of the *emes,* the real skinny, the true gen, this is the condition
to which most of us aspire. And here gossip is a sometimes dubious but often necessary resource. Carefully weighed, its origin
thoughtfully considered, gossip can connect the dots, fill in the

blanks, in otherwise incomplete and sometimes incomprehensible pictures.

In an example from public life, I recall being surprised in 1965 that Arthur Goldberg allowed himself to be persuaded by then President Lyndon Johnson to resign his seat on the Supreme Court to replace the recently deceased Adlai Stevenson in the post of American ambassador to the United Nations. The question any sensible person asked at the time was, Why would Goldberg agree to exchange one of the most distinguished jobs in the nation, one providing lifetime tenure, a full-salary pension, and an important role in the history of the nation, for a job of secondary importance where anything resembling permanent achievement was unlikely? The best answer I could come up with at the time was that Goldberg's willingness to make this switch could be explained only by the high-pressure salesmanship of Lyndon Baines Johnson.

Then the other day, in conversation with a journalist, Arthur Goldberg's name came up in some peripheral connection. I happened to mention that I never understood why Goldberg gave up his Supreme Court seat for the U.N. ambassadorship. "I know something about that," the journalist said. And she proceeded to tell me that an influential Chicago lawyer she knew, who was a good friend of Goldberg's, told her that Johnson wanted to give Goldberg's seat on the Court to his friend Abe Fortas, and he was able to get Goldberg to step down because he had something on him from his days in the labor movement. What it was that Johnson had on Arthur Goldberg she didn't know, so hers remains a tantalizing but still incomplete piece of gossip. Yet I find in it a more plausible explanation than the one that has Lyndon Johnson simply able to talk Goldberg out of his Supreme Court seat.

Some people seem to be magnets for gossip: the Kennedys, Princess Diana, Michael Jackson, Marilyn Monroe, the Clintons. Soon after Marilyn Monroe died—and before all the rumors of the cause of her death began to circulate—I mentioned to the novelist Saul Bellow, with whom I was friendly at the time, that I thought Joe DiMaggio, Monroe's second husband, seemed very grand in taking over the complex details of her funeral. "Yes," Bellow said to me, "but then of course when they were married, he used to beat her up fairly regularly, or so Arthur Miller [Monroe's third husband] told me."

Is this, do you suppose, true? Surely it's plausible. Joe DiMaggio was a very physical type; Marilyn Monroe was neurotic, self-absorbed, and doubtless difficult to live with. She presumably told Arthur Miller, who told Saul Bellow, who told me, who is now telling you that DiMaggio used to beat her up. Is this gossip or merely reporting something deeply unpleasant? Or is this a distinction without a difference?

Vanity Fair recently ran a story reporting that Arthur Miller had had a Down syndrome child with his third wife, the Swedish photographer Inge Morath. Soon after his birth, Miller clapped the boy into a less than first-class institution and didn't deign (I believe "deign" is the precise word) to see him ever again. The existence of the boy was revealed only after Miller's death, when it came time to divide his estate among his children, including this son, who was by then forty-one years old. Sorry though I feel for the son, I like this bit of gossip because it illustrates deep hypocrisy, and since the best gossip tends to be about hidden behavior, this qualifies, with four oak leaf clusters. The hypocrisy involved is that of Arthur Miller, a man always ready to offer moral lessons to others, to entire nations in fact, when he himself had done something in his personal life most people would consider morally repugnant. Miller often fell into a sermonizing mode. He was never uncomfortable instructing people how to live, or governments how to conduct their business. He spoke at all times with an unrestrained moral authority, dispensing advice on right conduct. Pity he didn't take that advice to heart with his own son instead of dispensing it so generously to the rest of us. All saints must be judged guilty before proven innocent, as George Orwell noted, and Arthur Miller, a false saint, fails the test.

I have told this story about Arthur Miller's conduct to seven or eight people. In doing so, I am not reporting a falsehood — *Vanity Fair*, if only out of fear of a lawsuit, would surely not run so damaging an article without thoroughly checking its facts—but am I nonetheless gossiping? I suppose I am, with the motive behind this particular piece of gossip little more than sweet Schadenfreude, the pleasure in catching the famous or the mighty in blatant hypocrisy. And hypocrisy, as Nick Denton, the founder of the gossipy website Gawker.com, likes to say, "is the only modern sin."

Another piece of gossip I have purveyed, though this one with some guilt, has to do with the drinking habits of the late Senator Daniel Patrick Moynihan. The gossip here comes in the form of a joke. The joke is that, when people phoned for Senator Moynihan, a drinking man, during one of his binges, one of his staff would say, with suppressed mirth, "The senator can't come to the phone. He's on the floor right now." I have told this story, too, a number of times, because I think it amusing. The guilt I feel at doing so is owing to my belief that Pat Moynihan was the most intelligent man in the United States Senate over the past half century, and the only one I can think of I would care to meet for lunch.

I never did meet Moynihan for lunch, but he is someone who contributed a few articles to a magazine I once edited, and who used to call me from time to time to chat about unpolitical subjects. The day I departed that magazine, he had a flag flown over the Senate in my honor—a flag that he subsequently sent to me and that is now in my son's possession. Yet I persist in telling that "He's on the floor right now" story. Why? Because, as I say, I think it amusing, and because I expect the people to whom I tell it will think me charming for passing it along to them. Such are sometimes the pathetic motives, and the even more pathetic rewards, of gossiping.

Along with showing one is in the know, another motive for passing along gossip is the assertion of superiority it sometimes allows. If someone tells you about the alcoholism of another man, isn't he also implying that he is himself without such a problem? If I report on the hypocrisy of another writer, writing one way and living another, as I did in my anecdote about Arthur Miller, am I not suggesting that my own life shows no such divide? If I recount another person's pathetic vanity, am I not also asserting my own common sense, levelheadedness, and refreshing absence of vanity? Behind much gossip, in other words, is often to be found, implicit though it may be, the claim of the superior virtuousness of its propagator. To seem both in the know and morally superior, all through the agency of gossip—not at all a bad deal, I'd say.

Diary

One day I had a call from a youngish man, a poet of middling-high reputation and achievement, who told me that he was about to be offered the job of chairman of the National Endowment for the Arts. Since I had been a member of the National Council of the NEA, he called to ask me what I thought of his taking the job. He prefaced his call by saying that he knew he should probably not take it, should instead continue working at his literary career. But, he added, he had long been afflicted with "a certain Jeffersonian sense of public service," which made the job tempting.

When he mentioned that "Jeffersonian sense of public service," I knew I was dealing with someone being less than straight with himself, so I strongly advised him not to take the job. "You know," I said, "a car and chauffeur come with the chairman's job. And my guess is that once you leave the job, you will miss the services of the chauffeur so badly that your life will never again seem as good."

Odd, but, ignoring my advice, he took the job anyway.

GREAT GOSSIPS OF THE
WESTERN WORLD, I

The Busybody

We know a vast amount of what went on in Versailles at the court of Louis XIV, especially between the years 1691 and 1723, when the French monarchy, having reached the apogee of its power, was descending and slowly wending its way to the murderous French Revolution. Much of what we know comes from a little man with a perhaps exaggerated sense of amour-propre named Louis de Rouvroy, Duc de Saint-Simon. From his coign of vantage at the middle distance from power, he sedulously took careful notes. In his retirement years, he turned these notes into the most extensive, richly amusing, gossip-ridden, and impressive memoirs ever written.

Some 1,500 people (servants included) lived within the walls of the grand palace Louis XIV built for himself and his courtiers, who were housed in 250 apartments of various sizes, many of them small and airless, but no less valued for that. Everything at the Versailles court was carefully ordered by rank, which was awarded by birth, an order that the King himself frequently subverted by placing power in the hands of the secondary nobility, the *noblesse de robe,* who became his mandarin bureaucrats, and in those of his mistresses.

Whatever one's position at court, all sought the favor of the King and those closest to him. Louis XIV was appropriately called the Sun King, for all the other planets and satellites of power revolved around him. Rivaling ambitions, with cabals forming everywhere, flourished. Jockeying for position at Versailles was as natural as breathing.

In his *Memoirs,* the Duc de Saint-Simon reports, in a spirit of candor and not less frequently spite, a great many things we couldn't have known without him; he goes into private matters about which he makes pointed judgments, rarely neglecting to provide interesting speculation about low motives. Even when they are wrong, the *Memoirs* are never stupid; even when they are angry, they are amusing.

Saint-Simon was barely five feet tall and walked the halls of Versailles perched upon red shoes with high heels and spoke in a squeaky voice. He frequently strikes a note of disapproval in his *Memoirs,* and took, it seems, only strong positions. He stood for purity of blood and seniority, loathed ruptures in tradition, especially when these entailed violations of the elaborate etiquette of privilege that was still for the most part in place under Louis XIV, though beginning to fall away under the regency that followed the King's death.

Saint-Simon complained, for example, about Te Deums being sung for people of lesser rank than the King and Queen, noting that "nothing now was sacred." He became exercised when mere members of the *Parlement,* an assembly of judges, were permitted to remove their hats in the presence of dukes and peers, of whom he was of course one. Those who in any way attempted to diminish or otherwise trample over his status became his enemies for life. (Saint-Simon's family peerage dated only from 1635, conferred on his father by Louis XIII; at the death of Louis XIV in 1715, he was himself the eleventh duke and peer in order of seniority.) Birth and rank were to him as sun and sustenance. Punctilious to a fault, a pedant of privilege, he everywhere made a great nuisance of himself by insisting on his full prerogatives as a duke.

One of the Duc de Saint-Simon's relentless complaints throughout the *Memoirs* is about the disreputable private life of his friend, subsequently the Regent, the Duc d'Orléans, who kept, and hugely enjoyed, company with courtesans and roués. Saint-

Simon was always trying to shape up the Duc d'Orléans, while never failing to record his lapses. Saint-Simon wasn't the only gossip at Versailles. Suppers the Regent gave for his cronies, the Duc notes, were wild gossip fests: "Everyone was discussed, ministers and friends alike, with a license that knew no bounds. The past and present love-affairs of the court and Paris were examined without regard for the victims' feelings; old scandals were retold, ancient jests and absurdities revived, nothing and nobody was sacred. M. le Duc d'Orléans played an active part in all this, but it must honestly be said that he seldom took much account of the talk."

The Duc de Saint-Simon deplored raucous, scattershot, motiveless gossip, or so he claimed. His own gossip tended to be subtle, well aimed, and (he would assure you) never out of line because of the purity of his own motives. No one was more *parti pris* than he. His never claiming otherwise is one of his attractive qualities. "Stoicism is a beautiful and noble chimera," he wrote. "It would be useless priding myself on being impartial."

The *Memoirs* provide much useful fodder for historians, but Saint-Simon was a grander writer than he was a historian. The greatest French novelists — Stendhal, Balzac, Proust — admired him, Proust even artfully lifting material from the Duc's memoirs for his own novel. Stendhal claimed that, along with eating spinach, reading the *Memoirs* was among his greatest passions. Saint-Simon was an original stylist — he apparently invented the words "publicity" and "patriot" — strong on invective, and especially fine on the analysis of character, much of the material for which he acquired by being attentive to gossip.

The Duc de Saint-Simon arrived at Versailles in 1691, at the age of sixteen, and in 1694 began keeping the notebooks that would result in his *Memoirs*. In his retirement he assembled and reworked these notes into the great book that he intended to be published posthumously. (The *Memoirs* were first published, in a poor edition, in 1788.) Whether he knew he was creating a considerable work of art is not known. What is unmistakable is that he intended his more than three-thousand-page work, forty-plus volumes in the standard edition, to be read by a posterity that would be sympathetic to his attacks on his many enemies and his self-justifications.

In his *Memoirs,* Saint-Simon claimed never to set down things he hadn't seen or heard at first hand or been told by what he took to be reliable witnesses. No one would view these *Memoirs* as in any sense objective, which doesn't mean that they aren't for the most part truthful. Saint-Simon had his positions—a grander name, perhaps, for prejudices—and they were manifold: his penchant for established hierarchy, rank, and tradition; his reverence for religion and genuine piety yet loathing of ambitious Jesuits, and his preference for those bishops who remained in their dioceses and took care of business and those who valued the contemplative more than the social or political life; his distaste for adultery, especially double adultery, where both parties were married; his contempt for homosexuality, seeing it as an effect of weak character and poor breeding (Louis XIV's brother, known as Monsieur, was homosexual); his impatience with stupidity; his dislike of greed; his respect for those who lived with a sense of their own achievements while recognizing their limitations; his unrelenting view of the comic preposterousness of men and women, never more so than when it came to their amours, many of which he learned about from Versailles' rich gossip grapevine.

"I resolved to let nothing escape me," Saint-Simon writes early in his *Memoirs,* and not too much did. His curiosity about how things happened at court was unquenchable, his search for motives unrelenting. At times he seems to operate as the ethnographer, the Malinowski, of Versailles, studying the strange habits of the natives residing there. At other times he is as caught up in the madness of life at the court of the Sun King as anyone else, as when, for example, he and his wife spent the astounding sum of 20,000 livres on their clothes for the wedding of the Duc du Boulogne, grandson of Louis XIV.

The Duchesse de Saint-Simon is perhaps the only figure in the *Memoirs* who is neither criticized nor gossiped about. She is repeatedly credited for her kind heart, her loyalty, the generosity of her sentiments. She was his one reliable confidante, and he often praises her sagacity. "What a great treasure," he wrote, "is a virtuous and sensible wife!" She frequently takes it upon herself to rein in this husband who, a bit of a hothead, is ready to desert Versailles and its many intrigues, or to calm him in his propensity for the rash act he is determined upon but she doesn't permit him to commit. They had three children: two dullish, disappointing sons, known at court behind their backs as "the dachshunds," and a daughter badly deformed by a crooked spine who had a taste for quarrels and made a bad marriage to a man interested only in her money.

The Duc de Saint-Simon was a gossip-historian. Gossip, the word and the act, comes into play throughout the *Memoirs*. "In the event everything becomes known at Court," he wrote, and the reason was that in the atmosphere of Versailles all knowledge was useful, especially against rivals. Ears and eyes were everywhere. A large number of people at court had a well-developed taste for gossip as sheer entertainment. Mme. de Clerambault, the daughter of the King's secretary of state, along with gambling "loved private and confidential gossip, and cared for nothing else." Attending physicians, priests, servants, everyone close to the King with the exception only of his horses, was a potential — and more often an actual — purveyor of gossip.

Perhaps the most avid recipient of gossip at Versailles was Louis XIV himself. The King, Saint-Simon notes, "was becoming more and more avid for information regarding everything that went on, and was even more interested in gossip than people imagined, although he was known to be vastly inquisitive." Gossip was the only way Louis XIV had of understanding all the intrigue around him. As the sole lever for raising or lowering the status of his subjects, the King depended on gossip to offset the persistent flattery that he also welcomed. Meanwhile everyone gossiped about the King. From Saint-Simon we learn, among a great many items about Louis XIV, that he slept with his mistresses in the afternoon and the Queen at night.

The extent to which Saint-Simon contributed directly to this fund of the gossip made available to the King we cannot know. The two men met in private audience only twice. Louis XIV thought well of the Duchesse de Saint-Simon, and often invited her and her husband to Marly, his country retreat. But he thought the Duc de Saint-Simon an argumentative man, difficult, altogether too obsessed with his rank, too critical of those who did not come up to his standard, too eccentric for his taste.

"Whom are you angry with today?" the Duc de Chevreuse once asked Saint-Simon. *Le petit duc* was never without his causes, his rivals, his enemies. The King's mistress and later his second wife, Mme. de Maintenon, he despised, referring to her, "his greatest obstacle," as "the old bitch"; elsewhere he calls her and the Duc du Maine "the ancient whore and bastard." Père Le Tellier, the King's confessor, he loathed. The Duc de Vendôme he thought little more than an intriguer and a vile power merchant. Although he revered the monarchy, he felt less than full reverence for the reigning monarch, for the King "had a rooted dislike and suspicion of men who were intelligent and well-informed, and that to be so considered was rated a crime in me." But, then, his "enemies said I was too clever, too well-informed, and took advantage of the King's fear of such qualities to put me out of his favor."

Saint-Simon wasn't, as we would say today, paranoid, but his strong opinions, the verbal violence that he found it difficult to curb, turned Versailles into a snake pit for him, with every snake carrying the venom of gossip against him.

Le petit duc was a species of busybody. Had you asked him, he would have said he was a busybody for the public good, for he had a strong sense of how the business of the nation of France, both within and without, ought to be conducted, and he did all he could to bring other people around to his way of thinking.

Saint-Simon felt that there were fights he couldn't get out of, intrigues he couldn't ignore, without losing his honor. It wasn't in him to "endure to swallow continual insults at the Court nor to adapt a servile pose which I despised." He knew, too, that his passionate nature gave him "the reputation of being a busybody, clever, experienced, full of malice."

One must possess an interesting, not to say strange, temperament to be able to spend the last decades of one's life polishing up a record of one's days that one chooses not to have published in one's lifetime. Why would anyone do that? To set the record straight, if only for posterity, is one possible reason. To have one's say—in many instances, in Saint-Simon's case, one's revengeful say—is another. Reading his *Memoirs* is like reading a sublimely fascinating gossip column. That the people being gossiped about are long dead scarcely deflects from the pleasure that such gossip provides, which is a tribute to the power of Saint-Simon's prose.

"Tact and prudence," Saint-Simon writes, "are not typically French virtues." Not to speak ill of the dead is a commonplace admonition that he obviously never considered, for he regularly speaks devastatingly ill of the dead. In the *Memoirs,* which are organized chronologically, whenever he announces at the top of a paragraph that a certain courtier has died, one knows one is in for brilliant, candid, and penetrating character analysis.

As one courtier after another dies, Saint-Simon sends him or her into the afterlife with a horseshoe floral arrangement of subtle criticism. The Duchesses de Villeroy was "honest, unaffected, frank, loyal and secret; despite her little wit, she succeeded in making herself redoubted at the Court, and ruled both her husband and father-in-law." Then there is Fenelon, the archbishop of Cambrai, "growing old beneath the weight of disappointed hopes"; La Chétardie, "the imbecile director, nay the master, of Mme. de Maintenon's conscience"; and let us not neglect La Fontaine, "who wrote the celebrated fables, yet was so boring in conversation."

Saint-Simon's best gossip, the dishiest of his dirt, is of course reserved for his enemies. He is relentlessly critical of the overreaching ambition of Mme. des Ursins, the supreme directress behind the ruler of Spain, Philip V, as Mme. de Maintenon was over the ruler of France, Louis XIV. Or consider the Duc de Noailles: "He is the very sink of iniquity, false-hearted and treacherous, making use of everyone. Scorning the commoner virtues, and serving only his own advantage, he is the most abandoned libertine and a bare-faced and unwavering hypocrite . . . An adept at lies and slander, if he is cornered he twists snakelike, spitting venom, using the most abject shifts to entice one back and crush one in his coils." And here he is on the son of Pontchartrain, the King's chief minister:

> He was of average height, his face long, with sagging cheeks and monstrous thick lips, was altogether disgusting, and deformed as well, since smallpox removed one of his eyes. The glass-eye that replaced it was perpetually a-weep, making his appearance alarming at first glance, but not nearly as frightening as it should have been. He had a sense of honour, but perverted; he was studious, well schooled in the work of his department, tolerably industrious and ever anxious to appear more so. His perversity, which no one had curbed or checked, permeated all that he did . . . If ever he did a kind action he boasted of it to such an extent that it sounded like a reproach . . . To cap all, he was mean and treacherous, and prided himself on being so.

This goes on for two more densely packed paragraphs, without any slackening in the intensity of Saint-Simon's lacerating, gossipy criticism. There are scores of such portraits scattered throughout the *Memoirs*.

Saint-Simon wasn't a putdown artist merely. When a person met his high standards, he could be handsomely complimentary. On the wife of Chancellor Pontchartrain he wrote that she "had that exquisite politeness that measures and discriminates between degrees of age and rank, and thus puts everyone at ease," and then goes on to cite her many good works. Or at the death of the dowager Maréchale d'Estrées he writes:

> People feared her; yet her company was much sought after. They said that she was spiteful; but if so, it was only through

speaking her mind freely and frankly on every subject, often with much wit, and always with spirit and force, and by not having the temperament to suffer fools gladly. She could be dangerous at such times, when she let fly with an economy of words, speaking to people's faces such cruel home-truths that they felt like sinking through the floor; but truly, she did not enjoy quarrelling or scandal for its own sake; she simply wished to make herself redoubtable and a person to be reckoned with, and in that she succeeded, living the while very happily with her own family.

In some ways the Maréchale d'Estrées sounds like a female version of Saint-Simon, who of himself writes, "I was never noted for restraint."

A believing Christian, Saint-Simon was nevertheless not notable for the virtue of forgiveness. He felt that one of the staggering weaknesses of his friend the Duc d'Orléans was that he pardoned his enemies, and thereby turned a virtue into a vice. He himself said that "God bids us to forgive, but not surrender our self-respect." He was an excellent hater, was *le petit duc,* who could say about his enemy the Abbé Dubois that "all vices fought for mastery in him, each continually striving and clamoring to be the uppermost."

And yet, for all this, the Duc de Saint-Simon was a good man. His own politics were without the major element of self-promotion. He wished only a wise and just administration directed by a fair and honorable monarch. He was to be disappointed in his desire. His influence over the Dauphin, the Duc de Bourgogne, was of course dissipated at the death of the young Dauphin. The Duc d'Orléans attempted Saint-Simon's plan of government by councils, but the members of the councils argued among themselves, and the plan, not aided by the Regent's tergiversations, fell apart. Lecturing, at times hectoring, the Duc d'Orléans as he did, people began to think Saint-Simon, as the historian Emmanuel Ladurie has it, "a tiresome bore."

"My influence ceased after the death of M. Duc d'Orléans,"

in 1723, the final year covered in his *Memoirs.* Apart from a brief run as emissary to the court of Spain—the expenses of keeping a personal staff while there nearly bankrupted him—Saint-Simon was no longer at, or even near, the center of things. He had "a conviction of my complete uselessness [which] drove me further and further into retirement." Toward the end he reports that he "no longer held any offices, and was living in almost complete retirement." Plush retirement, to be sure, in an *hôtel,* or mansion, in Paris and at the castle on his estate in the country. Yet it was not an altogether voluntary retirement: he was told by Fleury, the tutor to Louis XV and later that youthful King's chief minister, that his presence was no longer wanted at Versailles. Nothing left for *le petit duc* but to write his *Memoirs.*

All memoirs are, more or less, gossip. Hard to imagine a man so inquisitive, so critical, so penetrating, and with so many enemies as Saint-Simon not using gossip both as a means of self-justification and as a weapon against enemies. He wrote of his "passion for discovering, unraveling, and generally keeping up to date with intrigues that were always fascinating, and which it was often useful, and sometimes highly advantageous, to know." That he felt himself so embattled, with people against him on every side, left him always on the qui vive for an enemy's weakness, and gave him cause, as he himself put it, to "examine everyone with *my eyes and ears.*" The great nineteenth-century critic Sainte-Beuve called *le petit duc* "the spy of his century," and what is spying but a species of gossiping? Spies don't necessarily have to be in the pay of government; every first-class gossip is, when one comes right down to it, a spy in business for himself.

Saint-Simon claimed to write "the history of my own times, which, from the beginning, has been my sole purpose." He also reports that "you will find no scandals in these memoirs except where they are needed to explain the general situation," which is not true. He reports, to cite but one example of hundreds, of one Bentivoglio, a papal nuncio, that "he thought nothing of keeping an opera-singer, and of having two daughters by her, who were known to be such, and went by the nicknames of 'La Constitution' and 'La Legende.'"

In the end, it is the personal details, much more than the broad sweep of Saint-Simon's political or religious views or his general narrative, that make the *Memoirs* so enticing. Much of our pleasure in reading him derives from such items as learning that, when Peter the Great visited Paris and Versailles, "it did not suit the Czar or his staff to restrain himself in any way." Or in his telling us about a fellow named Arouet who "was sent to the Bastille for writing scurrilous verses," who was "the son of my father's notary," and that "nothing could be done with this dissolute son, whose rake's progress ended by his making a fortune under the name of Voltaire, which he took in order to conceal his true name." Or of the miser Pecoil, who dies locked in his own vault, contemplating his money. Or of the thoroughly unpleasant Marquis de Thury, felled by a leg of mutton wielded by the Duc d'Elbeuf at table, "leaving a permanent scar on his most unpleasing countenance, though at the time he did not retaliate."

Saint-Simon claimed his *Memoirs* were "authoritative and first-hand," which is so. He did not claim impartiality, for, as he puts it, "one is attracted by honorable and truthful persons; provoked by the rogues who swarm at Court, and made still more angry by those who do one harm." He was correct, too, in writing of his *Memoirs* that "none heretofore has contained so wide a range of subjects, treated more thoroughly, in greater detail, or combined to form so instructive and curious a whole." Gossip was never practiced with a surer hand or at a higher power than it was by *le petit duc,* who turned it into literature.

5

The Truth Defense

Men are children. They must be pardoned for
everything, except malice.

— JOSEPH JOUBERT

IN TURGENEV'S NOVEL *Virgin Soil,* a character named Valentina Mihalovna Sipyagina reports in a letter to her brother "an
'amusing' piece of news": she discovered that his friend Nezhdanov is in love with Marianna, her niece and the object of her
brother's love, and that Marianna, moreover, is in love with Nezhdanov. "She was not repeating gossip," Turgenev recounts Valentina Mihalovna adding, "but had seen it all with her own eyes and
heard it with her own ears. Markelova's [her brother's] face grew
dark as night." What Valentina Mihalovna writes to her brother is
factually true; and it is true, too, that she really did witness what
she reports. Does the truth factor, then, justify Valentina Mihalovna's claim that she is not indulging in gossip?

Is truth a defense in gossip as it is in libel cases in the United
States? If one is telling something that, though it has all the other
components of gossip, is true, does it cease to be gossip and instead become that more dignified phenomenon, information?
Things would be much less complicated if it were, but it isn't.
Just because something is true does not indemnify the person
who passes it along from the charge of gossiping; just because it is

true doesn't mean it isn't also gossip. In gossip, intent counts for a great deal—sometimes for everything.

In the example from Turgenev's novel, Valentina Mihalovna dislikes her niece Marianna and has not had her own usual success in charming Nezhdanov, her son's tutor. She is, strictly speaking, telling the truth, but she obviously takes much more pleasure in the truth she has to tell than simply passing along information normally brings: by telling her brother this sad news, she is also diminishing in his eyes his friend Nezhdanov and the woman he loves, thus scoring points off both. Valentina Mihalovna is, in a game she is entirely aware of, happily throwing the darts of gossip. Malice here is aforethought and brings her genuine pleasure; and it is this mixture of malice and the pleasure she takes in it that is behind the gossip she brings her brother. Pure gossip it is, malevolent division.

When Tina Brown's book about Princess Diana, *The Diana Chronicles,* was published in 2007 more than one reviewer mentioned the romance novelist Barbara Cartland's speculation, reported in Brown's book, on the breakup of Diana's marriage to Prince Charles: "Of course," Miss Cartland said, "you know where it all went wrong. She [Diana] wouldn't do oral sex." The old admirable English reticence is apparently done for; in England fellatio, or the absence thereof, is being spoken about openly, and by the upper classes. But more to the point, is what Barbara Cartland reported true?

What led her to this gaudy speculation? One possible motive is that she wasn't invited to Diana and Charles's wedding, because, Tina Brown recounts, she and her daughter Raine were deemed too garish for so grand an event. But motive aside, how could Cartland know whereof she spoke? Might Princess Diana have told her about this little problem she had? Might, much less likely, the Prince of Wales have lodged a complaint with her about his wife, or in her presence? Might it have been someone whom one or the other told and who subsequently told Cartland, who then told Brown? (The notes on sources in *The Diana Chronicles* do not help on this point.) Might Barbara Cartland, the author of more than seven hundred novels of the sort known as bodice rippers, and hence a woman not without sexual imagination, have made it up? Whatever the case, as a gossipologist one has to admire the aesthetic perfection of the item itself, suggesting as it does a certain girlish squeamishness in the young princess, a brutishness in her older husband.

The item has everything, featuring as it does the Prince and Princess of Wales, two of the most prominent face cards in Europe. Terribly intimate it is, too, about as intimate as gossip can get. Does it have the feeling of plausibility? A sophisticated woman I mentioned it to said she doubted it. "Diana was a very modern girl," she added. But it is a bit of gossip that does not admit of certainty—it can be neither proved nor disproved—and its very uncertainty makes it all the richer.

Such is the extreme candor—or is it utter want of reticence?—of the times in which we live that people often gossip freely about themselves and people they claim to love. The actress Angie Dickinson told the author of a profile of her that ran in the January 2008 issue of *Vanity Fair* that she had a ten-year love affair with Frank Sinatra, the great secret about which is that neither was really crazy about the other; the deepest passions of both were not engaged. They apparently used each other as, in effect, relief stations. "There's a difference," Miss Dickinson says, "between having to have something and wanting something."

Did Angie Dickinson want John F. Kennedy, with whose name hers has also been linked? In the same *Vanity Fair* profile, she remarks on her distaste for Paul B. Fay, a friend of Kennedy's writing about his and her relationship in his book *The Pleasure of His Company*. Because of her distaste for such gossip about her and Jack Kennedy, we are told, she turned back a six-figure advance to write an autobiography, though she had completed more than a hundred pages, with "all the details intact." In other words, Angie Dickinson seems to be saying, she did have an affair with the president but prefers not to talk about it, at least not in any detail—or is it not at these prices? "I didn't want to let it go out," she tells her interviewer. "They wouldn't believe me if I said it never happened . . . Anyway, it's time for everybody to grow up about the Kennedys. It's more important what we lost as a country." Thus do gossip and patriotism live comfortably side by side.

One view of gossip holds that when it isn't motivated by revenge, it is motivated by egotism and status needs. All the bits of gossip recounted in this chapter can be explained by this view: Barbara Cartland's in her account of the failure of the royal marriage comes across as an insider; Angie Dickinson's in her interview with a journalist comes across as a woman who has been intimate with two of the most powerful men of her time. Might my own gossip from the previous chapter, the items about Joe DiMaggio and Daniel Patrick Moynihan, not also be charged up to status needs, for each involves the act of name-dropping—specifically, my dropping the names of Saul Bellow and Pat Moynihan, claiming a relationship with both? Thus do gossip and snobbery also live comfortably side by side.

Not all gossip need have motive. Some gossip is passed along out of sheer exuberance, with no greater motive than the desire to entertain one's friends. One brings a delicious bit of gossip in the same spirit that one brings a bright new joke, to lay at the feet of people whose point of view is roughly congruent with one's own and who are therefore likely to enjoy it. Not all gossip has a punch line; only some of it is amusing; but both gossip and jokes have in common that they begin with the question, Did you hear this one? (W. H. Auden said that "Did you hear this one?" ought to be the motto for psychology and the head trades generally.) Both enterprises, gossiping and joke telling, suggest the world is less predictable than one might have thought, for a joke whose outcome one can predict is no better than a bit of gossip one already knows.

The notion of gossip as disinterested information, not always having a deep or dreary motive behind it, is suggested by Jacob Klein, in his day a famous teacher at St. John's College in Annapolis, Maryland. In his essay "The Idea of Liberal Education," Klein referred to gossip as "the soft underbelly of knowledge," calling it "the small tribute that our passionate and appetitive life pays—in very, very small coins—to intellectual life." Gossip may seem chiefly to have to do with idle curiosity, but it can also spark serious curiosity. "It must be granted," Klein wrote, "that it is not always easy to draw the line between idle curiosity and this nobler kind of curiosity." Reading this, I am reminded that, in his splendid biography of the philosopher Pascal, Morris Bishop complains that "gossips have told us too little" of Pascal's daily affairs.

A severe definition of gossip might be that of passing along information that is really nobody's business. But who is to say what does or does not fall into this broad category? A man or woman without any interest in gossip may be impressive in his or her restraint, but also wanting in curiosity, uninterested in the variousness of human nature, dead to the wildly abundant oddity of life, and thereby, in some central way, deficient.

Diary

When my friend Hilton Kramer was the principal art critic of the *New York Times,* from 1965 to 1982, he was a fount of wonderful gossipy stories about the idiocies of its various editors and reporters, most of them having to do with their self-importance.

One such story had to do with a famous *Times* columnist who, during the Vietnam War, had recently returned from Hanoi to the paper's London bureau, where Hilton was at the time, covering some art events in England. Hilton had just learned that there were serious storms in the American Northeast, with a real possibility of flooding in Connecticut, where he had left his wife alone in their house in Westport. When the *Times* columnist saw Hilton, he noted his worried look. Hilton explained it was there owing to his concern about the prospect of flooding in Connecticut. "Oh," said the columnist, "I've just returned from Hanoi, and after seeing what I saw there, I must say, flooding in Connecticut strikes me as pretty trivial stuff."

"Moral prig," Hilton thought, "arrogant bastard," but he said nothing.

Three days later, Hilton ran into the columnist again, who was now himself looking worried. When Hilton asked him what was troubling him, he said that he had just heard that there might be flooding in Virginia, where he had a house and family. Hilton considered holding back, but then couldn't resist. "Oh," he said, "maybe you ought to return to Hanoi, where you can easily take your mind off such trivial stuff."

6

The Gossip Transaction

Gossip is like a butterfly, namely, the more you chase it,
the more it will fly away from you. If you sit still,
it will land on your shoulder.

— FILIPINO SAYING

IN YIDDISH, a *yachneh* is a coarse, loudmouthed woman,
while a *yenta*, only slightly less odious, is a gabby, talkative
woman, a blabbermouth. Do *yachnehs* tell gossip to *yentas*,
who then spread it around where it can do real damage? Or is it
the other way around, *yentas* to *yachnehs?* How does gossip get
going, and what keeps it alive?

A good joke, they say, requires three people: one person to tell
it, another to appreciate it, and a third who doesn't get it. Gossip,
too, needs three people: one person to initiate it, another to hear
it and (perhaps) pass it on, and a third who is its subject or victim.
But gossip also needs a setting, a basic understanding among the
gossipers, an agreement about what is of interest in the vast array
of the world's information.

The origin of the word "gossip" is in the designation of a god-
parent for one's child, the person designated being a "god sib,"
or relative made through religion. More important, this godpar-
ent status implied a closeness, an intimacy, so that the god sib is a
man or woman in on a family's inner workings and hence some-

one very much in the know. Another etymology of the word, variously attributed to General George Washington and others, is connected with Washington's instructions during the Revolutionary War to American spies to "go sip" with the enemy in taverns and learn what their military plans are. "Go sip" could also refer to the gossipy talk that goes on in coffee klatches. (*Klatsch* is the German word for gossip.)

One does not gossip with just anybody. A person purveying gossip has to show some discrimination in choosing an audience for his gossip. That person — or persons — must be someone who roughly shares one's view of the importance or the amusement of the information being passed along to him. He must inhabit the same general realm of interest, of temperament, of taste. One doesn't tell a scandalous story about a three-star French restaurant to the guy at the Jiffy Lube, nor does the guy at the Jiffy Lube tell the suburban gourmand about the rich female customer he has been bonking for the past four months while her husband is busy earning $1.6 million a year at his white-shoe law firm.

The person conveying the gossip also has to be reasonably certain that the person he is telling it to is ready to receive it. If one is thoroughly pleased with one's ophthalmologist, one is probably not eager to hear how he supposedly botched five conventional cataract surgeries. If one adores a coworker, one is, similarly, less than delighted to learn that she badly neglects her young children and is filing for bankruptcy.

No matter how deep his delight in gossip, the originator of it must never seem as if he worked hard at acquiring the information he is passing on. He might want to stress its exclusivity (no one else knows this) or its intrinsic importance (this can strongly affect your fate), but he must avoid the appearance of seeming to have done any serious sleuthing to come into possession of the item he is now vouchsafing to you. Were he to do so, he would come across as that most miserable of creatures, a damned busybody. The difference between the busybody and the gossip, at least to the onlooker, may come down to little more than style and sang-froid, with the busybody not having much of either.

The person receiving the gossip has to stake out his position with some nicety. He mustn't seem preternaturally interested in what might be salacious, slanderous, or generally scandalous material, lest he resemble the man in the tan raincoat coming out of the pornographic movie theater at 3 p.m. At the same time that he must appear somewhat cool at the reception of the gossip, he is also under the obligation to seem appreciative. When hearing the item, he must measure its truth quotient, and know how to respond to it. Sometimes he may wish to prompt more information from the person purveying the gossip, wanting gaps in the narrative filled in, foggy points in the story clarified, contradictions resolved.

A complicated transaction, then, that between the person telling the gossip and the person to whom he is telling it — a dance of a sort, really. A quid pro quo is also often entailed. If you regale me with two enticing items of gossip, oughtn't I to come up with at least one for you? "Gossip," the satirist Wilhelm Busch, in an admirable aphorism, said, "is the confession of other people's sins," which it frequently enough is. But to accept gossip from another person is also to enter into intimacy of a complex kind: the bestowal of the gossip along with its acceptance implies the acknowledgment that we are both men or women of the world, both operate in the same moral universe, both find the same things funny, outrageous, insuperable.

Although almost all gossip speaks to one or another form of moral contamination, by no means does all gossip require the response of moral indignation. My own preference as a recipient of gossip is for items that feature the comedy of human behavior: the comedy, that is, of people trying to live up to their own probably too high pretensions. The best gossip for me is that which confirms my own views of the essential fraudulence of certain people, especially people who present themselves as a touch — and usually more than a touch — more moral than the rest of us. Thus I reveled in the gossip a number of years back, subsequently printed without denial in a national magazine, about the intellectual who found everyone whose political positions did not agree with his own morally contemptible, but who was himself discovered to be stealing and selling review copies of books from the magazine he worked for to support a cocaine habit.

Good gossip is much aided by the existence of a human typology, by which slightly obscure formulation I mean that gossip is best when it demonstrates people acting not merely badly but to type. In the story earlier told about the *New York Times* columnist freshly returned from Hanoi, the type is that of the Hypocrite Virtucrat, the person professing virtue without really possessing it. The item I reported earlier about the painter who did not know who Dick Cheney was demonstrates the type of the entirely Self-Absorbed Artist. Other happy types, all hardy perennials, are the Old Lecher, the ignorant Culture Vulture, the Social Climber, the Secret (or Not So) Drinker, the Aging Hippie, the Oblivious Wealthy, the Happy Philistine, and many others. Such types resemble the characters in a medieval morality play. Gossip about them almost always satisfies.

Diary

I wasn't particularly nuts about J. V.'s first wife. She was tall, stately, handsome rather than beautiful, but too intense for my taste, especially about politics, at which she had worked professionally, fundraising for local and statewide candidates. She could be rebarbative, frosty, off-putting. From the middle distance, which is as close as anyone viewing other people's marriages can hope to get, J. V., after some years of heavy drinking early in the marriage, seemed reasonably content with his wife.

Then she was discovered to have cancer. Her death was a slow one, with lots of false hope along the way, adding that extra touch of torture that cancer brings to so many of its victims still in midlife. I had lost touch with J. V. during those black days, though he must have come through all right, for he remarried, in his middle fifties, to a woman about whom everyone who met her said was a dear, dear person, kind and generous. My friend J. V. had apparently swum into safe harbor.

Much though I liked J. V., I saw him only infrequently, and I never met his new wife. Along with her reputed sweetness of character, she was supposed to have been wealthy. J. V. had himself done well, and retired early. So there they were, two very nice people, neither of whom had children, who had found each other, living out their days together without known complications, a happy ending, or as close as one gets to one in this life. Or so everyone thought, until J. V. turned up in California, the word among his friends being that his idyllic marriage was over.

The question of course is Why? Behind that question an expansive field of gossip opened up. Was J. V. drinking again? Was he cheating on her? She on him? Did they argue about money, even though they were thought to have more than a sufficiency between them? The possibilities are endless.

A friend told me that J. V.'s new wife suffered from depression. But so do lots of people, and I find it difficult to believe that J. V. would leave someone he had married late in life for a condition he must have known about before he married her. Then another friend, who is bipolar, reported having dinner with her, and he revealed that she takes the same drug he takes for his bipolar condition. Bipolarity is not easy to live with, not only for the persons who suffer from it but for those close to them. Might it be that the many problems that his second wife's bipolar condition brought on proved too much for J. V., who was in his mid-sixties when the marriage broke up and who might have looked forward to spending his final years sailing calmer waters? Possible.

Now yet another friend told me that the wife of a friend of his, who grew up with J. V.'s second wife, told her that she, the second wife, complained that J. V. had done her out of lots of money in the divorce. This seemed to me highly unlikely, for not only was J. V. himself wealthy, as I've mentioned, but he was not a man for whom money seemed to mean very much. He was also thoroughly honorable. Did his second wife really say this? If not, what would be the motive for someone else saying it?

What was going on here? The need for speculation is irresistible. And speculation leads naturally to gossip, which can be completely stilled only by an accurate, convincing, and finally true explanation of what happened, which is never going to be offered. And besides, let us not fail to remember, it's really no one's goddamn business.

7

Need Gossip Be Trivial?

What they [certain readers of fiction] want is "the story behind the story." It's gossip that they want. The thrill of the voyeur. To be told what really happened to you in your life rather than what you subsequently wrote about in your books. To be finally informed, without any window dressing or bullshit, who really did what with whom, and how, and how much. Give them that and they're happy. Give them Shakespeare in love, Thomas Mann telling all . . .

— AMOS OZ

EVERY PERSON'S LIFE may be said to exist on three levels: how the person's life seems to people who know him from the middle distance (his neighbors, coworkers, tradesmen he deals with), how he seems to those who are close to him (his family, his dear friends), and finally how he seems to himself. Some among us want all three versions, or at least to come as close as we can to acquiring all three.

"The version of ourselves we present to the world," wrote the English writer William Donaldson in his diary, "bears no resemblance to the truth. If we knew the truth about each other, we could take no one seriously. There isn't one of us could afford to get caught. That's all life is. Trying not to be found out." Gossip, of course, tries to find out.

Some of us, while zealously wishing not to be found out, none-theless want to find out all we can about others. "Enquiring minds want to know," the low-swinging *National Enquirer,* our very own leading American gutter-press rag, once blared in a popular television ad. Despite the source, the sentiment is true: enquiring minds really do want to know what people are truly like. Often they want to know what the people they regularly deal with are like; sometimes they want to know what historical figures were like. Was Virginia Woolf anti-Semitic, Leo Tolstoy a wretched husband? How is it that the capacious Winston Churchill, with his immense appetite for work, cigars, whiskey, and talk, seemed to be happy with one woman? Are these trivial questions? I don't happen to think so. Such information speaks to character, and the correct judgment of people the world deems important is itself significant.

The rap on gossip is not only that it can be mean, which it certainly can be, but that it is also trivial. The English novelist Ian McEwan has called novels "the higher gossip." What makes it higher is that one of the things novels attempt to do is show us human character as it views itself, in all its grandeur, illusions, joy, sadness, and not least secrets, some of which people won't even confess to themselves. At its highest level, gossip is after something similar.

Nor must one discount all the brilliant people who have not merely enjoyed but adored gossip. Take, for example, Sydney Smith (1771–1845), the clergyman who was one of the founders of the *Edinburgh Review.* Locked away for much of his adult life in country vicarages, Smith yearned for news of the great world, and gossip was his chief mode of acquiring it. He was in correspondence with some of the most clever women of the age, to one of whom he wrote, "Refresh my Solitude with Rumor's agitations." To another he wrote, "I am panting to know a little of what passes in the world." And to yet another, "I long to know the scandal." To Lady Mary Bennett, he implores, "Pray send me some treasonable news about the Queen . . . and don't leave me in this odious state of innocence, and make me as wickedly instructed as yourself." He understood that in the realm of gossip it is important to give if one is to receive. To Lord Grey he wrote: "I will send Lady Grey the news from London when I get there. I am sure she is too wise a woman not to be fond of gossiping; I am fond of it and have talent for it."

And here is Sydney Smith delivering the goods with his characteristic light touch to J. A. Murray, who worked on the *Edinburgh Review*: "As I know you love a bit of London scandal learn that Lady Caroline Lamb stabbed herself at Lady Ilchester's Ball for the love of Lord Byron, as it is supposed. What a charming thing to be a Poet. I preached for many years in London and was rather popular, but never heard of a Lady doing herself the slightest mischief on my account." If one panned gossip the way one pans gold, this particular item would constitute a perfect nugget. Lord Byron, for God's sake, now that's a name worth gossiping about!

As Sydney Smith well understood, candor, where possible spiced with humor, is the proper conversational note for gossip. When gossiping, people are presumably leveling with each other; it will not do to hold back, or appear to hold back, or seem to make the other party tease the information out of one. Part of the delight of gossip, after all, is, to use an old-fashioned word, its naughtiness. One is telling tales out of school, tattling, hanging out dirty linen, blowing the whistle, doing all sorts of things one isn't supposed to be doing. Engaged in such activities, it is no time to hang, or hold, back. "And another thing . . ." is one of the most welcome transitions known to lovers of gossip.

Gossip is only truly trivial when it descends too low—too low not in content so much as in subject. When I was a teacher at Northwestern, I had an acquaintance who used to call me to report on the foolish behavior of certain colleagues about whom I hadn't the least interest. "Gossip about X is lower than I wish to go," I would tell him, forcing him to desist, "especially at eight-thirty a.m." Only as I write this last sentence does it occur to me that one of the meanest things one can say about another person is that one finds him intrinsically too uninteresting to be worth gossiping about.

Diary

I was at lunch with a young critic who had put together a book of essays about Lionel Trilling, perhaps the most subtle and penetrating American literary critic of his day. I asked him if in connection with his book he had had any contact with Trilling's wife, Diana. He said he had met with her a few times. "She was crazy, you know," I said, which got his attention.

Some time after her husband's death, Diana Trilling wrote a memoir called *The Beginning of the Journey,* in which she described her husband as a depressive with a drinking problem. In the book, she also described her husband's bouts of unexplained fury, frequently directed toward her.

Portions of a diary Lionel Trilling kept were also published, earlier, in the magazine *Partisan Review,* in which Trilling reveals that he felt himself something of a fraud as a teacher because he had no genuine scholarship, knew no foreign languages. What he really had wanted to be was a novelist, but, though he published a single novel called *The Middle of the Journey* and a few short stories, something kept him back from risking a career writing fiction. This conflict, of living one kind of life and longing for another, is, in the conventional view, thought to be the reason for Lionel Trilling's depression.

Later, in 1999, Trilling's son, James, published an essay in which he asserted that his father suffered from attention deficit disorder. James Trilling had ADD, and he claimed to find all the major symptoms of this mental problem also present in his father: the disorganization, the inability to finish things begun, the unwillingness to make clear decisions, the rage — all the symptoms that he, James, had found in himself.

But, as I told the writer sitting across from me, I wonder if the real source of Lionel Trilling's problem wasn't depression or ADD but his marriage and family life. Both Diana and Lionel Trilling were devotees of psychoanalysis, and Diana was a genuine neurotic: afraid of heights, afraid of crowds, and a person easily slighted, touchier than an open wound. When her still quite young son James, her only child, was afraid of elevators, she wrote to the psychoanalyst Erik Erikson to report that she thought what the boy was truly afraid of was what the elevator represented to him: the dark embrace of the vagina.

I then went on to describe her behavior as a member of the editorial board of the *American Scholar* when I was its editor. Her performance was that of the outrageous diva, all temperament, no rationality whatsoever. A friend told me that she stopped reading around 1957, and when I knew her, in the middle 1970s, there was no reason to dispute this. This didn't stop her from pontificating about nearly everything in the culture. She once ruined an editorial board meeting by rattling on pointlessly about an anodyne article on her husband in the magazine. No one could stop her. She would sometimes call me with ridiculous requests. She was preposterous. "Nuts," I said, "she was plain nuts."

"My point," I told the young writer, "is that Lionel Trilling's problem probably wasn't that he was doing work that, though it brought him great prestige, he didn't really believe in. His problem was that every night of his adult life he went home to this nutty woman, and to a son who had his own problems. No, Trilling was depressed for the reason that he had married the wrong woman and stood by her through, you might say, thin and thin, and it must have weighed on him terribly. No wonder he was depressed, no wonder he drank, no wonder he would fall into rages directed at their proper target, his wife. He had made an enormous mistake in marrying Diana, and it destroyed his life."

Was this, I asked myself as *I* went rattling on, setting the record straight or gossiping about the dead? Since it is both derogatory and speculative, my guess is that most people would find it the latter. Which only goes to show that not even death provides a release from being gossiped about.

8

Pure Speculation

The sorrows of our heroes and heroines, they are your delight,
oh public! their sorrows, or their sins, or their absurdities; not
their virtues, good sense, and consequent rewards.

— ANTHONY TROLLOPE, *Barchester Towers*

EPISTEMOLOGY, THE DICTIONARIES tell us, is the investigation of what distinguishes justified belief from mere opinion; it also has to do with the theory of knowledge. Gossip is indisputably a form of knowledge. The chief question about it, always, is How reliable a form of knowledge is it?

Some gossip is based on discernible facts, hard evidence, from which people can go on to construct more or less interesting hypotheses about the behavior of a person or the meaning of an event. A woman leaves her husband is such a bit of hard evidence; she is gone, moved out. Another hard fact is that she has moved in with another woman. Here the speculation that is intrinsic to gossip begins. Has she moved out because of mistreatment on her husband's part? Or has she moved out because there is someone she loves more than him? As for her moving in with another woman, is this merely a stopgap arrangement? Has she, that is, moved in with a friend until such time as she can get her own apartment and her life back in order? Or is the friend more than a friend, in fact a lesbian lover?

Some years ago, precisely this story was brought to me about a friend, someone I didn't see often but liked a lot, a woman who lived in another city. My own reading of the hard evidence was that her husband probably was brutish, and that she, who was then in early middle age and had two grown children, had moved out into the apartment of a female friend until she could set things up on her own. After all, I concluded, if I had to move out of the apartment lived in by a wife from whom I was separating, there was every chance that I would, temporarily at least, move in with a bachelor friend. I thought any other reading of these events was pure gossip. In the event, I was quite wrong. My friend, after more than twenty years of marriage, had decided she was lesbian, and lesbian she has happily remained. The moral of the story, if moral there be, is that more daring speculation was called for; things were not as on the surface they appeared; and a commonsense explanation turned out to be the wrong one.

The act of speculation is itself hedged all around with personal sentiment—or, to use the less euphemistic term, bias. I recently read the memoir of a writer named Ann Birstein, who was the third wife (of four) of the literary critic Alfred Kazin. Their marriage of thirty years was tempestuous, and that is putting it gently. Birstein published her memoir, *What I Saw at the Fair,* in 2003, five years after Kazin's death, and it chronicles all of the couple's domestic storms, hurricanes, monsoons.

Ann Birstein's book is motivated, I do not think it going too far to say, by hatred for her former husband, a hatred grounded in deep disappointment and it is no doubt justified. She was a novelist married to a powerful literary critic who seems never to have expressed any appreciation, or scarcely any interest, in his wife's writing. Twelve years older than she, he was more experienced, more in demand, more famous. He was also inconsiderate of her own ambition to the point of cruelty.

But all these things, unpleasant enough in their way, are as nothing compared to Birstein's claim that her husband used to beat her fairly regularly, sometimes with sufficient force to knock her to the floor. "We'd be making love. I'd be happy. Then Alfred would suddenly say that I didn't know how to do it, and fly into a rage. During other arguments he would rip the sleeves out of my bathrobe . . . or tear at my hair, which the next day I would comb out in bunches. Always after these episodes, Alfred would cry, say he had never hit any other woman but me."

This information, if true, makes Alfred Kazin not merely a brute but a sick brute. It also makes for very rich, if also repulsive, gossip. I say "if true," but is there any reason to doubt its truth? One reason might be resentment on Ann Birstein's part. Hers has not been a glittering literary career; her published novels have not caused much comment. While married to her, Alfred Kazin could have helped gain attention for them, but didn't in the least bestir himself to do so. Birstein has a more general complaint. She is a feminist, whose feminism takes on the heavy freight of victimhood, so that reading her one senses her feeling that much of the failure of her career is owing to a system badly rigged against women writers.

What we have in Ann Birstein, as they might say in a courtroom, is a hostile witness. You also have in me an all too credulous juror, for I thought Alfred Kazin a creepy character before reading his third wife's account of his bullying brutishness. What made Kazin creepy, I always thought, was his confident presentation of his own superior virtue. No matter what he wrote about, he always seemed to position himself as better than his subject and his audience. He made himself seem the only man who understood the true meaning of the Holocaust, the only man who knew the importance of radical thinking in America, the only man genuinely worried about nuclear war, the only man who kept his own purity when everyone around him was selling out. On his left, the red hordes; on his right, the Black Hundreds; in the middle, one good man, standing alone, you'll never guess who: Alfred Kazin. So it is all the jollier, all the juicier, to discover that this self-proclaimed good man was a wife beater, and a weepy one at that.

Why did Ann Birstein wait until her husband's death to defame him so enthusiastically? Perhaps she feared direct revenge when he was alive. (When Philip Roth's second wife, the actress

Claire Bloom, wrote about what a wretched husband and stepfather Roth was, he responded by drawing a crushingly cruel portrait of her in a thinly veiled novel called *I Married a Communist*.) Perhaps, who knows, she feared more beatings, or litigation. But she has given that small portion of the world that cares about her and her dead ex-husband much in the way of richly vicious gossip to contemplate, and I now seem to be passing it along.

The rise, some have called it the triumph, of psychotherapy in modern life has provided people one more subject—along with sex, money, and moral hypocrisy—about which to gossip: that of a person's psychic state. As amateur therapists, gossips analyze other people for their psychological weaknesses, not to say deformities. "She's very insecure," two people might casually say about a third. Or "He's obviously paranoid." Or "His relationship with his mother has always been fundamentally skewed." Or "She exhibits all the behavior patterns of the nymphomaniac." All this kind of talk, even in the hands of a professional therapist—and "therapist," if you insert a space after the *e,* spells "the rapist"—is pure speculation. In the hands of a gossip, it can also be speculation with intent to wound.

If much of gossip is speculation, almost all of it requires interpretation. One must examine a piece of gossip as one would a novel; the more subtle the gossip, the more subtle the interpretation needed. Some gossip is crude, its intention obvious, and no training in literary criticism is required to unpack its meaning. Other gossip can be Proustian in its subtlety, and calls for refined interpretation.

Nearly all human acts outside the most basic ones call for interpretation. One recalls here Metternich, the great Austrian diplomatist who, when informed that the Russian ambassador would not be attending the Congress of Verona because of his death, asked, "I wonder why he did that?" Not all speculation need be as cunning as Metternich's, but certain incidents, events, and bits of randomly acquired information call forth speculation of a kind aligned to gossip. "Perhaps the urge to participate in gossip comes from knowledge of the impossibility of knowing," writes Patricia Meyer Spacks in *Gossip,* her study of the connections between gossip and literature. "We continue to talk about others precisely because we cannot finally understand them."

Speculation is nearly inseparable from gossip. One sees a married man in what appears to be intimate conversation with an attractive woman much younger than he, and one must, it strikes me, speculate on who she might be and what is the nature of their relationship. One has a neighbor, a man in his forties, who doesn't seem to go to work yet lives exceedingly well: travels frequently, dresses expensively, has tickets to lots of concerts and other cultural events. What is he living on? An inheritance? A trust fund? Earnings from something illicit? A woman in her early thirties has had a number of affairs with men her age, living serially with them for extended periods. She has often talked about wanting children but is not ready to do so without a husband. What is it about her that has made finding a husband, at least thus far, impossible? Invitations to gossip, under the banner of speculation, all of these.

It may well be that our married man with the younger woman is in reality meeting his attractive niece, the young man living large with no visible means of support is a skilled day trader, the woman in her thirties with serial lovers has less wrong with her than is wrong with so many men in midlife who are terrified of commitment. It may well be, in other words, that all one's gossipy suspicions were flat-out wrong, proving that a dirty mind never sleeps but perhaps from time to time ought to.

But is it a dirty mind or, less balefully, a merely curious one that invites such speculation? Encountering unconventional or ambiguous behavior, one naturally seeks an explanation for it. The search often requires knowledge of facts that are unavailable, which leaves one having to settle for speculation about these unknown facts.

Curiosity—"one of the lowest of the human faculties," E. M. Forster said—more often than not trumps honor, and does so most frequently in the form of gossip, which in turn is ready to betray secrets, circulate slander, and violate privacy, all to satisfy the beast of curiosity. At any sophisticated level, curiosity operates under the assumption that appearances and reality are usually very different, and gossip, often with the aid of daring speculation, sets out to fill in the discrepancy between the two. Sometimes it does so accurately, sometimes mistakenly yet charmingly, and sometimes meanly and disastrously. But whatever its intention, whatever its subtlety or want of subtlety, whatever its effect, whether it issues out of envy or voyeurism, revenge or the desire to entertain friends, gossip will not be suppressed.

II

PUBLIC GOSSIP

9

Gossip Goes Public

Gentlemen, if you continue to publish slanderous pieces
about me, I shall feel compelled to cancel my subscription.

— GROUCHO MARX to *Confidential* magazine

ONCE A LEISURE-TIME pursuit, an activity carried on
between individuals in the agora or the forum or the
drafty halls of Versailles or (much later) over the backyard fence in small towns, gossip officially went public with the
advent of the printing press, the rise and spread of literacy, and
the resulting proliferation of newspapers and journals, most of
which were only too pleased to carry it. Once print, in the form
of journalism, became available to larger and larger segments of
every national population, gossip ceased to be entirely a mouth-
to-ear private transaction and became more and more a public business. Gossip itself soon became professionalized: people
made their livelihood by gathering and spreading it.

As this happened, gossip also became strangely impersonal-
ized. The best gossip, as far as the gossip writers were concerned,
wasn't about the family next door, but about the famous: royalty,
the rich, politicians, successful artists, great athletes, and, in our
time, movie stars. But before gossip in the newspapers became
democratic breakfast fare for the family, it had to overcome considerable resistance from people who valued their privacy. For at

the level of journalism, gossip is, always and everywhere, an invasion of privacy.

Gossip has played a central role in many eighteenth- and nineteenth-century novels. But the first novel in which, in its professionalized role, it occupies a central place is *The Reverberator* (1888), one of Henry James's lesser novels on the subject of his international theme: Americans abroad in their exchanges with Europeans and their older, more complexly layered culture. The Americans in the novel are one of those solid but unsophisticated, invariably well-to-do families, the Dossons, from Boston, consisting of a father and his two daughters on an extended visit to France. In the early pages, the Dossons are accompanied around Paris, shown a few of the velvet ropes, by a go-get-'em American named, appropriately, George Flack, who is a society reporter for a newspaper in the United States called the *Reverberator*.

Far from being in any way ashamed of his work, Flack feels he is on to a very good thing, the coming thing, the Next Big Thing in fact. He tells Miss Francie Dosson, on whom he has romantic designs, that the paper for which he works is "a big thing already and I mean to make it bigger: the most universal society-paper the world has seen. That's where the future lies, and the man who sees it first is the man who'll make his pile. It's a field for enlightened enterprise that hasn't yet begun to be worked." Flack before long will demonstrate how far he is willing to go to work it. He also believes that privacy is dead, and remarks: "It ain't going to be possible to keep anywhere out of the light of the press. Now what I'm going to do is to set up the biggest lamp yet made and make it shine all over the place. We'll see who's private then."

Flack learns that the Dosson girls have made a connection with the Proberts, an older American family that has been living in France since the time of Louis-Philippe, who was King of France between 1830 and 1848, and have assimilated themselves entirely to French culture. He sets out to get the Proberts' story and write it up for the *Reverberator*. He will subsequently be aided in this plan when Francie Dosson becomes engaged to young Gaston Probert, and, in her American innocence, blithely tells Flack everything he wants to know about the exclusive Probert family, including the fact that one of its members suffers from klepto-mania.

Francie supplies Flack with precisely what he wants: "genuine, first-hand information, straight from the tap." He, as his job requires, goes on to write it up for the *Reverberator*'s large American audience. When word of this unwanted publicity gets back to the Probert family, they are devastated. As Mme. de Brécourt, one of Gaston Probert's sisters, puts it, "Everything is at an end, we have been served up to the rabble, we shall have to leave Paris." The story is the old Jamesian one of two sets of people operating under different standards, of conduct: the Europeans greatly value their privacy, and the Americans don't quite see the problem in losing it.

The working out of the plot is of less interest—Francie Dosson and Gaston Probert do, after much fairly conventional Sturm und Drang, marry—than the mechanics of gossip illustrated by the story. As Delia, the other Dosson sister, says, not so much in defense as in explanation of the behavior of George Flack: "He says that's what they like over there [in America] and that it stands to reason that if you start a paper you've got to give them what they like. If you want the people with you, you've got to be with the people." All too true, as the history of American and British journalism has borne out. Between the privacy that dignity requires and the publicity that newspaper reading requires, privacy goes down to defeat nearly every time.

The issue—publicity (sometimes justified as the public's right to know; sometimes, as in the United States, dressed out in the First Amendment, guaranteeing freedom of speech) versus the privacy requisite for reasonable dignity—remains central to this day, and is unlikely to disappear soon.

As recently as the summer of 2008, an English court dealt with a lurid case in which it came out favoring privacy over publicity. Max Mosley, the sixty-eight-year-old son of Oswald Mosley, the leader of Britain's fascist party during World War Two, a man made wealthy by his clever promotion of Formula One auto racing, was discovered enacting sexual fantasies with five prostitutes. The women were wearing Nazi uniforms, and film captures Mosley participating in, among other activities, a mock lice inspection of his hair and spanking one of the prostitutes, counting off the number of strokes in a German accent.

Not, let us agree, everybody's idea of a good time, but sexual wackiness has always been a staple of the British gutter press. "Never underestimate the appetite of the English for prurient sexual gossip," the critic Robert Gottlieb noted. But in the instance of Max Mosley this wasn't a matter of the gutter press stumbling on his sporting activities; in fact, the incident was set up by a tabloid called *News of the World,* which not only hired one of the prostitutes to film the fetid festivities, with a camera the size of a sugar cube hidden in her bra, but also offered her $50,000 to write it up. The paper printed the story under the front-page headline "My Nazi Orgy with Fi Boss."

The case of Max Mosley versus *News of the World* is another of those disputes in which one's own antipathies are evenly divided. Mosley, as it turns out, won the case, the judge deciding that, uncomely though his taste in sexual games might be, it did not involve an element of criminality, and hence to expose it to the public was viewed as a violation of Mosley's right to privacy. The case is thought to have set a precedent in England for more stringent enforcement of privacy laws. Whether or not it will remains to be seen.

So much in the realm of gossip remains to be seen. Sometimes "remains to be seen" can ruin a career. On August 7, 2008, the *New York Times* printed a lengthy front-page story with the headline "Accusations of Sex Abuse Trail Doctor," with the subhead of "Advocate for Students—He Issues Denial." The story itself, which runs for sixty-three column-inches and contains a color photograph of the physician and another of the back of the head of one of his accusers, recounts in squalid detail the charges against the physician. A pediatrician specializing in helping children who don't do well in school, the accused wrote successful books on the subject. He also happened to have one of those perfect résumés: Rhodes scholar, Harvard Medical School graduate, *New York Times* best-selling author, highly thought of in his field. He denied all the charges against him.

Which didn't stop the *Times* from rehearsing the charges in lavish detail. He was supposed to have given physicals to boys between the ages of five and thirteen in which, in their nakedness, he touched their private parts; he was also supposed to have asked them the contents of their nocturnal emissions. "Dr. X [as I shall call him] would always examine [her son's] testicles while [his] penis touched or was very close to the doctor's cheek," the mother of one of the plaintiffs averred. Five of his former patients, now men, filed lawsuits against him. They were represented by the powerhouse attorney who had sued the Boston archdiocese in the case against sexual abuse by priests.

One can feel the effort of the *Times* reporter straining to be fair, to tell both sides of this story: a number of the accused physician's colleagues were quoted on his behalf, remarking on his good character and the importance of his work. But isn't the true question, Should such a story be told at all? Why not let it work its way through the courts and then report on the verdict? In his novel *The Last Puritan*, George Santayana has a character who was accused of a crime, and later acquitted, say, "Being acquitted is nothing in this world. Being accused is what makes all the difference." The only reason for telling the story of the respected pediatrician was perhaps the fear that someone would come along and tell it before the *Times* did—the fear, in other words, of being scooped. As it stands, the article was really little more than gossip, and, owing to its sexual content and its potential consequences, most unpleasant gossip. The story was, finally, ruinous. Even if the doctor is found not guilty in court, his reputation will be destroyed, in good part owing to this article. He will always be the man about whom those nasty stories were told—and told in no less significant a place than the *New York Times*.

What gives this sad tale a touch of piquancy is that while the *New York Times* was going to press with it, it was laying off a much larger, in the gossip term much juicier, story: that of the extramarital affair of John Edwards, John Kerry's running mate for the presidency in 2004 and himself a presidential candidate in 2008. Perhaps one reason the paper ignored this story was that, a few months earlier, it had been burned printing a piece with insufficient evidence about Senator John McCain, then running for president, having an affair with a campaign worker. The apparent reason that the *Times* steered clear of the Edwards story was probably not the paper's often-cited liberal bias, but more likely its provenance in the *infra dig National Enquirer,* which had been on John Edwards's trail for a long while, accusing him not only of conducting an affair while his wife had cancer, but of fathering a child with his illicit lover, accusations that proved to be true.

In the end, the squalid *National Enquirer* got it right and the earnest and prestige-laden *New York Times* got it wrong. The *Times*'s "public editor," who is hired to sit in judgment of the everyday running of the paper, concluded that the *Times* was incorrect to fear slumming, by taking up a story first unearthed by a gaudy tabloid. Meanwhile, one of the paper's assistant managing editors, Richard Berke, apropos of the paper's dilemma in going after hot, gossipy stories such as John Edwards's behavior provided, said: "We run the risk of looking like we're totally out of it, or we're just like the rest of them—we have no standards."

Yet a greater question is at stake. Why worry about slippage in standards when it comes to hypocritical politicians and then have no hesitation about possibly destroying a serious medical career? Such has been the pervasiveness of gossip, and its extension in our day to all departments of life, that the question of standards in journalism has become more slippery than the cavorting of a sleek, philandering politician.

Diary

I was among the people awarded an honorary degree—my only such degree, and I neither want nor expect nor need another—at a university of no great distinction. My most notable fellow honorees were the choreographer Agnes de Mille, the writer Cynthia Ozick, and a documentary filmmaker. I remember very little about the latter except that he had a young—much younger than he—beautiful, and kindly wife. Over drinks, I told a trustee of the university, in what I hope was not a lascivious way, that this young woman (she was French, as was the filmmaker) seemed dazzling. "Oh," said the trustee, a man in possession of the lowdown on every artist and intellectual on two continents, "you mustn't be in the least envious of him. For ten years he had to sleep with Simone de Beauvoir. So he has, you see, earned every moment with his charming young wife."

10

Gossip Goes Center Ring

Gossip is no longer the resource of the idle or
the vicious, but has become a trade, which is pursued
with industry as well as effrontery.

— LOUIS BRANDEIS and SAMUEL D. WARREN,
"The Right to Privacy"

S OMETIMES, THERE'S NEWS IN THE GUTTER" was the condescending headline of the public editor's piece on the *New York Times*'s failure to pick up the adultery story of John Edwards, the item on which the previous chapter closed. I write "condescending" because, as anyone who reads the daily press and watches television cannot fail to recognize, journalism, electronic and print, is itself everywhere more and more in the gutter. The day on which I write this, the *Times* has a small item in its Arts section about the actor Richard Dreyfuss suing his father and uncle for return of an $870,000 loan he made them in 1984. Why is that, in a serious newspaper, news, and what does it have to do with the arts? Isn't this a matter among Dreyfuss, his family, and the law courts, and distinctly not that of the *New York Times*?

Apparently not, at least not so long as Richard Dreyfuss has achieved modest celebrity in his career as a movie actor. Because of the way we now live, Dreyfuss is probably better known to lots of Americans than people who live down the block from them in the suburbs or one floor below them in an urban high-rise. One of the dubious rewards of celebrity is that strangers become interested in aspects of your private life that, strictly speaking, are none of their business.

How this came about is a long and complicated story. Let us consider a drastically shortened version, limited to the spread of the professionalization of gossip only in Britain and America. It begins, as noted earlier, with the rise of printing in the late seventeenth and early eighteenth centuries. The growth of literacy soon enough created a hunger for news, and the news for which new readers hungered most was that of the bad behavior of their betters.

Grub Street, as the lowlife journalist fraternity in England collectively was known, was quick to supply this demand. As early as 1681, a London newspaper reported a ménage à trois with a woman, her maid, and her dog, a large mastiff. After 1695, the Licensing Act was revoked, which put an end to censorship and stimulated the advent of more newspapers, many of them purveying scuttlebutt, much of it of a scurrilous sort. Daniel Defoe, author of *Robinson Crusoe* and *Moll Flanders,* was among the writers who trafficked in this realm, and was himself placed in the public pillory (for three days, in 1703), thence to Newgate Prison, for publishing libelous material. Richard Steele and Joseph Addison's *Spectator,* much read in the coffeehouses of London, a paper that stakes a claim as genuine literature and survives to our day, also appeared in these years, the beginning of the second decade of the eighteenth century, and it, too, went in for gossip.

Many of the new specialists in gossip, Defoe among them, camouflaged their victims by describing them but not mentioning their names. Much of this new journalism divided itself by political party, with Whig publications digging up dirt about Tories, and Tory publications doing the same with Whigs. Then there were the calumniators who worked gossip for purposes of blackmail, threatening to release damaging information about a person unless he or she agreed to pay to suppress it. (In *The Devil in the Holy Water, or The Art of Slander from Louis XIV to Napoleon,* Robert Darnton has shown how a similar operation was at work in France.) Retaliation could be vigorous. The professional gossip in those days had to know how to use his fists and be an adept duelist.

With the spread of literacy to the lower classes, the great subject for gossip, in those days as in ours, was the wretched behavior of the rich and wellborn, going from royalty on down to patricians, simple gentry, writers, and actors. The point, for the readers of such stuff, was to show that one's betters weren't, at bottom, really any better at all; they were rather worse, actually, perhaps no surprise given that they had more money and more gracious margins of leisure along which to behave badly.

Female readers supplied a new audience for gossip, and their news interests were not always the standard ones of politics and crime. They preferred the details of everyday and of private life, with a special interest in the so-called polite world and its denizens: who was seen with whom at assemblies, playhouses, operas, and the rest of it. Naturally, anything scurrilous that could be turned up was a bonus, and as such much welcomed.

James Boswell, author of the *Life of Johnson,* put in his days as a gossip columnist, and wrote some seventy columns under the name "The Hypochondriack," between 1777 and 1783, for the *London Magazine.* In his excellent book *Scandal: A Scurrilous History of Gossip,* the English writer Roger Wilkes recounts Boswell's subject matter, which ran from public hangings to the soup-swilling habits of Scots lairds. Very little that was human was alien to Boswell, who was himself a grand carouser and whoremonger, which gave him a natural instinct for gossip. This he supplied to his readers, like the gossip columnists of our day, in short, chatty paragraphs.

Later, Charles Lamb wrote gossip paragraphs for the press. Charles Dickens hired one of the first women, Lady Blessington, who was a member of the nobility, to supply gossip items for his newspaper, the *Daily News.* William Hazlitt, having been made the victim of gossip by the Tory press, strongly disapproved of gossip; so did Anthony Trollope. And Henry James loathed it, at least in its public version, though he gained much good material for his stories from private gossip picked up at the tables of the rich, with whom he often dined in London and at their country estates.

The nineteenth century, Roger Wilkes notes, ushered in the "age of personality in journalism." The advent in 1814 of the steam-powered press, making it easier to print great numbers of newspapers, gave gossip an additional boost. Readers wanted the inside story, which meant the personal story behind events. The personal story meant the details of private lives. Creating sensations became as important to the mission of the press as conveying information—best of all was information that made for sensation.

Suddenly in the gossip paragraphs of the racier English press lesbian relations were hinted at, as were ill-timed pregnancies and intemperate drinking and bad debts. The human-interest story began to suffuse newspapers, and what could be more human than the private lives, with a heavy emphasis on their miscreant behavior, of the rich and famous. Judgment was implicit in all personal gossip. Gossip writers ultimately set themselves up as judges of character. In the 1930s, the English critic Cyril Connolly would refer to "the gossip-writers who play Jesus for twenty-five pounds a week," but such writers got their start a full century earlier.

In America, the first gossip columnist was Benjamin Franklin, who under the heading "Busy-Body" in his own newspaper ran whatever items he could dig up about the foibles of folk in Philadelphia and beyond. "As most people delight in censure, when they are not the objects of it," he wrote, "if any are offended by my publicity exposing their private vices, I promise they shall have the satisfaction, in a very little time, of their good friends and neighbors in the same circumstances." Rather boastful talk, this, and as it turned out, Franklin failed to deliver on his promise, and his gossip column soon petered out.

In the realm of public gossip, America had over Britain the advantage, as mentioned earlier, of more lenient libel laws. Truth was a defense against libel in America, which means that if the person committing the libel believed the libelous statement to be true, he could mount a defense against litigation; if a person who felt himself libeled could prove that what was said about him, in print or (later) over radio or television, was untrue, he would win a lawsuit, with appropriate fines and punishment to follow. In England, a plaintiff feeling he had been libeled need not prove that what was said about him was untrue but prove only that the libel had damaged his professional, business, or family life to cause him to win damages. In England, therefore, you can tell the truth about someone and still be guilty of libel.

Such go-go, given-them-what-they-want American newspaper publishers as James Gordon Bennett of the *New York Herald,* the man who sent Henry Stanley to Africa to find Dr. Livingstone, pressed home this advantage by running interviews with celebrities and profiles about their lives at home. Americans who considered themselves well bred in the late nineteenth and early twentieth centuries had nothing to do with such stuff. John D. Rockefeller, for example, hired a public relations man, Ivy Lee, whose main job was to keep his name out of the press.

Soon it became evident that the best stories were those that people didn't want out in the open. (Here we return to our earlier definition of gossip as something someone doesn't want known.) The hottest subjects for gossip were those who were most vulnerable — those, that is, with the most to hide. America, however, did not have an aristocracy through whose peepholes gossip columnists might profitably gaze. But it did have an ever-replenishing plutocracy, whose children were notable for marrying badly, drinking incontinently, acting stupid generally. A rising celebrity class, created by newspapers to begin with, came into being. This class increased vastly when, with the aid of newspapers, there was less and less connection between achievement and fame; a celebrity became, in Daniel J. Boorstin's formulation, someone known for his well-knownness. Newspapers, even serious ones, understood that if they were to stay in business they must not only inform but entertain. And not many things were thought more entertaining than gossip about the rich, the wellborn, and the celebrated.

Some gossip writers felt that they were in fact offering moral instruction. A Civil War hero who fought at Gettysburg, Colonel William d'Alton Mann arrived in New York in the late nineteenth century and published a sheet called *Town Topics.* He claimed he printed gossip "for the sake of the country," adding that the people he wrote about were "an element so shallow and unhealthy that it deserves to be derided almost incessantly." Later, Nigel Dempster, an English gossip columnist, remarked about his own discovery and spread of gossip about politicians that they much deserved to be exposed, since they were all "liars, cheats, and fools," a point not easily disputed.

Curiosity about wealth itself became a regular feature of American gossip columns. A columnist named Maury Paul, who wrote under the name Cholly Knickerbocker for William Randolph Hearst's *New York American,* specialized in this realm. He coined the term "café society" to describe those wealthy and celebrated people, chiefly living in New York, who conducted their social lives in the tonier clubs and restaurants of Manhattan. For Paul and other gossip writers, the increase of divorce among the wealthy and celebrated enriched the content of their columns.

In England, many of the people who themselves might once have served as subjects of gossip became purveyors of it. The wellborn Nancy Mitford, daughter of Lord Redesdale, supplied gossip for British newspapers. Later, Winston Churchill's son, Randolph, would do the same. A man named Patrick Balfour, who went to Eton and thence to Oxford, wrote gossip about his contemporaries, the so-called Bright Young Things, who also became the subjects of the early novels of Evelyn Waugh. In America, Igor Cassini, the brother of Jacqueline Kennedy's designer Oleg Cassini, took over the Cholly Knickerbocker column, and through his Kennedy connection had lots of inside dope to peddle to his readers. He coined the phrase "jet set," which became the replacement for café society.

A strange change had meanwhile taken place: people in fast sets, in both England and America, began to crave being gossiped about; their names in the gossip columns reassured them of their own importance, or at least of their own with-it-ness. They befriended the columnists, who had become celebrities in their own right and who found themselves invited to the dinners and parties, to make sure that everyone there received proper mention in the next day's columns.

One of the most successful of the twentieth-century British gossip columns was that written under the pseudonym William Hickey, and one of the most readable scribblers to work under the Hickey name was Tom Driberg. Driberg was uncomplicatedly, even militantly, gay, very left wing, and a spy for the Soviet Union; he may also have been a double agent. The people he wrote about and by and large trashed, the so-called smart set, were fine fodder for his Marxisant views — look what swinish people capitalism has turned up now — simultaneously amusing and stirring up class hatred in his readers. The only rule he followed was that laid down by his boss, Lord Beaverbrook, owner of the *Evening Standard* and *Sunday Express,* in which Driberg's columns appeared. The rule was "All fucking is private," so sex wasn't to be mentioned in the column, which may on balance have been a good thing, since Driberg himself was more than once picked up for propositioning men in public lavatories.

Lord Northcliffe, founder and owner of the *Daily Mail,* defined the essentially gossipy nature of contemporary news: "what people talked about in kitchen, parlour, drawing room and over the garden wall: namely, other people." In the realm of gossip, England had over the United States the advantage of the royal family and their antics. Various Princes of Wales seemed to specialize in outrageous behavior, beginning with Queen Victoria's son, later Edward VII, a man who passed the decades waiting for his long-lived mother to die by entertaining himself with several mistresses. His grandson David, by all accounts a very boring man, made the hottest gossip writer's item of the twentieth century by giving up the throne for Wallis Simpson, an American divorcée of less than obvious charms, physical or spiritual. More recently the gossip writers have been able to feast on the current, and also very long-standing, Prince of Wales, Prince Charles, who seems to specialize in saying unfortunate things. His divorce from his wife, Diana, who was herself expert in disposing the gossip writers in her favor, gave the tabloid press one of its greatest field days of all. Whether Charles and Diana's sons, William and Harry, will, to the gossip columnists' delight, be scandal-prone remains to be seen.

By the late 1930s, American movie stars had become great magnets for gossip. The Hollywood gossip beat was divided between Louella Parsons and Hedda Hopper—with Jimmie Fidler and Sheilah Graham (F. Scott Fitzgerald's great good friend) comprising the second team—though both women were, in effect, in the pay of the movie studios, and released gossip of a kind that would titillate interest in, but rarely set out to destroy, the valuable property that movie stars had become. Hopper and Parsons also tried to enlarge their compasses to take in world affairs, à la Walter Winchell, but neither was ever able to bring it off. In their day, though, their power was genuine. "Only Hollywood," David Niven wrote in his memoirs, "could have spawned such a couple, and only Hollywood, headline-hunting, self-inflating, riddled with fear and insecurity, could have allowed itself to be dominated by them for so long."

The leading gossip sheet of the 1950s was the magazine *Confidential,* published by a man named Robert Harrison, whose background was in girlie, or so-called one-hand, magazines. *Confidential* specialized in Hollywood shenanigans, the raunchier the better. The magazine ran stories on Frank Sinatra's presumably prodigious sexual appetites, Robert Mitchum's pot smoking and other antics, Desi Arnaz's philandering, Sammy Davis Jr.'s passion for blondes, and the secret gay lives of ostensibly heterosexual romantic leads, Rock Hudson among them. Some of the stories in *Confidential* were true, some possibly true but not provable—no one has ever worked out the truth-to-falsehood ratio in this magazine that everyone scorned and nearly everyone felt he or she had to read. Only a series of exhausting lawsuits caused its eventual demise.

The 1960s changed the nature of gossip in the press. Things began gaudily with the Profumo Affair of 1963 in England, in which John Profumo, a cabinet member of the Tory government, was shown to be connected with prostitutes and Soviet spies in a way that was thought to compromise national security. From a professional gossip's point of view, the scandal had everything: aristocratic country estates, luscious hookers, international intrigue, kinky sex as only the English can do it. The Profumo Affair had much to do with bringing down the government of Harold Macmillan and elevated the interest in gossip as reported in the press. But long before this, nearly every large-circulation newspaper, British or American, felt it could not function without a gossip columnist.

In the United States, the *National Enquirer* picked up the scandal-mongering flag and ran with it—as it continues to do in our day. Paying for its stories and for insider photographs—cash on the barrelhead, and serious sums, too—it came up with relentless stories about secret love affairs, homosexual outings, AIDS roll calls, and much more. It supplied full-court coverage of such American sad freak shows as the death of Elvis Presley and the murder of O. J. Simpson's wife and her boyfriend.

People magazine, Time Inc.'s entry into the field, started out to be gossip with a friendly face. The original plan was to feature the private lives of public people, but with the emphasis more on intimacy—that is, on the genial private lives of celebrities—than on exposé. Soon other entrants joined the field—*Star, Us, Life & Style, In Touch, OK!, Rolling Stone, Vanity Fair*—and turned up the heat on *People*. No more Mr. Nice Mag, now it, too, goes in for dishing the dirt on celebrities wherever it can find it.

But the larger problem, the one with which this chapter began, is how straight-up, no-apologies public gossip has infected standard, or what once might have been called respectable, journalism. More and more newspapers such as the *Washington Post* and the *New York Times* are given over to stories that are little more seducing free-born boys and married women, Nero raped the Vestal Virgin Rubria . . . Having tried to turn the boy Sporus into a girl by castration, he went through a wedding ceremony with him—dowry, bridal veil, and all—took him to his palace with a great crowd in attendance, and treated him as a wife. A rather amusing joke is still going the rounds: the world would have been a happier place had Nero's father Domitius married that sort of wife."

Are such stories about Tiberius and Nero and other wild emperors true, or is Suetonius conveying only gossip? If it is gossip, it is assuredly of a high-quality sort. Suetonius feels it right to report these stories, if only to fill in his portraits of Roman rulers. But here is a case—and there are many such—where history and gossip blur, so that one cannot with certainty know which is which. Oscar Wilde called journalism organized gossip, and sometimes the same may be said of history, at any rate where it deals with undocumented material. The two, gossip and history, often blend into one.

Emperors, kings, and their wives and families long served as the main source of what we would regard as gossip. But in the eighteenth and early nineteenth centuries, warrior emperors and royalty began to be supplanted by raffish behavior on the part of the merely wellborn. Lord Byron is the stellar example. Though his accomplishments as a poet were genuine enough, he was also a celebrity in a way that no other poet has ever been. George Gordon Noel Byron, the sixth Baron Byron, was a man of talent, courage, wealth, and appetite. In a painting in which he wears the headdress of Greek independence fighters, whose cause he joined in their war against the Turks at the end of his life, he resembles the roguishly handsome Errol Flynn. Of his one physical flaw, a clubfoot, one can only say that on him it looked good, almost, in his day, making a limp fashionable.

Like the best subjects of gossip, Byron was a man about whom almost nothing could be disbelieved. Lady Caroline Lamb, one of his many lovers, famously called him "mad, bad, and dangerous to know." Gossip had him pegged variously as bisexual, com-

than gossipy in their intent. The earnest-seeming television show *60 Minutes,* with its celebrity interviews and political and corporate exposés, is increasingly gossipy in its impulse and interest. Television news generally, with its headline-and-pictures approach to the news, much of the time resembles nothing so much as tabloid raggery. Everywhere one looks in show business, politics, even business, gossip creeps more and more into the foreground. Once the freak show in journalism, gossip has now become center ring.

Diary

So Marlene Dietrich, in Washington to pick up an award from the Jewish War Veterans for her wartime work with Jewish refugees, pays a call on John F. Kennedy at the White House. She is shown into his private rooms. A bottle of wine is in a cooler. The president walks in, shows her the view from the balcony, says that he hopes she is able to pay a leisurely visit. Actually, she tells him, she has only an hour or so. "That doesn't give us much time, does it?" says Kennedy, and with that he leads her down a corridor and into a bedroom. He promptly begins undressing. (Later, Dietrich recalled his unraveling rolls of bandages, there to shore up his bad back, from around his body.) In bed, it is all over fairly quickly, and the leader of the free world promptly falls asleep. Dietrich soon wakes him, reminding him that she has to be at the gathering of two thousand Jewish veterans. Wrapping himself in a towel, he accompanies her down the corridor to an elevator, where he says, "There's just one thing I'd like to know." When she asks what it is, he replies, "Did you ever make it with my father?" She tells him that she did not. "Well," he says, "that's one place I'm in first." They never saw each other again.

II

Shooting at Celebrities

We live in an age when private life is being destroyed. The police destroy it in Communist countries, journalists threaten it in democratic countries, and little by little the people themselves lose their taste for private life . . . Without secrecy, nothing is possible — not love, not friendship.

— MILAN KUNDERA

WITHOUT CELEBRITIES, PUBLIC gossip would be impossible. But the world has never for long been without celebrities, and therefore not without public gossip either.

Perhaps the first great subject of public gossip, at least in the Western world, was the dashing Alcibiades (c. 450–404 B.C.E.), the Athenian who, during the Peloponnesian War, switched sides at least twice before finally defecting to the Persians; promoted the Athenians' fateful expedition to Syracuse, but did not lead it because he was thought to have defiled statues of the gods; was said to have been magnificently handsome and physically talented, a grand seducer of men and women alike, the man Socrates chose not to sleep with when Alcibiades offered himself to him on the night that the Platonic dialogue called *The Symposium* takes place — the subject, Alcibiades, of unending rumor and gossip, all of it richly fascinating.

The next great subject of public gossip was probably Alexander the Great. The chief bit of gossip about Alexander, of course, was that he was a god, gossip that the young Macedonian leader, who died at the age of thirty-three, did nothing to discourage. He may have come to believe it himself. Alexander had the press clippings of Achilles, without the dark temper, and the curiosity of Odysseus, without ever losing sight of the main prize, the domination of the known world of his day, which he achieved. "Alexander," writes Leo Braudy, in his history of fame, "deserves to be called the first famous person." Alexander not only had fame; he also cultivated celebrity, which in this sense means the assurance that one's fame is widely disseminated. He traveled with artists, who cast coins with his face upon them and made and erected statues of him in warrior poses. He named numerous, freshly conquered cities Alexandria and Alexandropolis. Unlike Julius and Augustus Caesar, he neglected only to name a month after himself.

How active a role gossip played among the Romans of the empire — that is, at the time of the emperors — cannot with exactitude be known, but from Suetonius (c. 69–130), the chronicler of the Caesars from Julius to Domitian, we get a strong sense that it was exotic and never in short supply. As men with unabashed power, emperors were likely to go in for strange and unchecked behavior, not a little of it lascivious, and this Suetonius recorded with happy enthusiasm. "On retiring to Capreae," he writes of Tiberius, "he made himself a sporting-house, where sexual extravagances were practiced for his secret pleasure. Bevies of girls and young men, whom he had collected from all over the Empire as adepts in unnatural practices, and known as *spintriae,* would copulate before him in groups of three, to excite his waning passions." In the paragraph following this, Suetonius writes, "Some aspects of his [Tiberius's] criminal obscenity are almost too vile to discuss, much less believe." Suetonius nevertheless goes on to describe them: "Imagine training little boys, whom he called his 'minnows,' to chase him while he went swimming and get between his legs to lick and nibble him."

Suetonius does no less in this line for Nero: "Not satisfied with mitting incest with a half-sister, producing illegitimate children, sodomizing choirboys. Wherever he went, Italy, Spain, Greece, his presence caused a stir, one of the side effects of which was a serious case of roundheels in attractive women. Everything about Byron was dashing, not least his verse, so much of which has been taken as autobiographical. "He was not merely a poet," as one of his biographers, Frederic Raphael, wrote, "but also a star, the first modern celebrity, the artist as performer and publicist."

In a brilliant career move, Byron died young. While working in Greece to help outfit the Greek fleet using his own finances, he had what were thought to be two epileptic seizures; a week later, he caught a cold, was leeched by his physicians, and, after slipping into a coma, died on April 19, 1824, at the age of thirty-six. His heart was buried in Messolonghi, Greece, and his body was returned to England, where it was refused burial in the Poets' Corner of Westminster Abbey, his life having been considered too scandalous to have been accorded such an honor. Byron's funeral cortege was attended by thousands, many of them working class, who became so overcome by emotion that they were said to have been near rioting. Such a display shows the early birth of the cult of celebrity, and celebrity is inevitably linked to gossip. Even today, nearly two centuries after his death, reading about Byron one feels that one is still in the grip of steamy gossip.

Byron was truly lordly, and the English, in the realm of gossip, have been fortunate in having an aristocratic class to supply them with touches of grandeur in this realm. Madcap dukes, drunken earls, knights for whom once a night and with a single sex were never sufficient. The current Prince of Wales, Prince Charles, the man who should but probably never will be King, has shown, through his marriage and subsequent divorce and remarriage, that British royalty is even now an ever-yielding source of the richest zany gossip.

Americans, as I mentioned earlier, have had no such unending resource as an always decadent aristocracy to fall back on for loopy gossip, and we have had to go at things in our own, at first less glamorous, way. In the early days of the republic, politicians were our only national celebrities, and so gossip formed around them, as of course it continues to do in our own time. Politicians are subject to gossip because they have power and, having power, are likely to abuse it by stealing, sexual excess, intemperance, or egregiously jolly hypocrisy. Much political gossip, like celebrity gossip, is about someone, because of his or her fortunate or favored position, going too far. Part of the pleasure in reading it—of seeing the miscreant nailed—is in viewing the mighty fallen. But part of the pleasure, too, is reading or hearing about people with more power than we possess using it to live in outrageous ways that the rest of us are for the most part restricted to dreaming about.

Political scandal has never been scarce. The intimate relationship between Thomas Jefferson and his slave Sally Hemings is a gift that, as they say about guilt, never stops giving. A good bit of gossip in Jefferson's day that has not yet died out in our own, the Jefferson-Hemings story trails on, with books continuing to be written about it and prizes given to some among those who write them. From there the beat goes on: Andrew Jackson's wife lived with him before divorcing her husband; there was talk of James Buchanan being gay; Lincoln was thought to have "Negro" blood, as Franklin Roosevelt was later to be thought Jewish; Grover Cleveland was rumored to have an illegitimate child, and it was whispered that one of his children, his daughter Ruth (after whom the candy bar Baby Ruth was named), was retarded. Gossip had it that Teddy Roosevelt was a heavy boozer and that Woodrow Wilson was a chaser of women. Warren Harding's love affairs in Marion, Ohio, were much gossiped about, and Eisenhower, as did FDR, really did have love affairs while in the White House. Adlai Stevenson was rumored to be both gay and a sedulous skirt chaser, a notorious heterosexual.

Very little of this got into the press. Scuttlebutt is what it was, passed around by word of mouth, thought to be the *emes,* the real McCoy, the inside story. What we now call the mainstream press had, or at least thought of itself as having, too high a standard to engage in innuendo and undocumented gossip about politicians' private lives. When the mayor of New York Jimmy Walker was, as we would say nowadays, sexually very active, he made no attempt to hide his various dalliances, the most notorious being with a British showgirl named Betty Compton, whom he later married. But the New York press, charmed by Walker and his refusal to revert to the least duplicity in these matters, gave him a pass and no one wrote about them.

John F. Kennedy was another politician given a free ride by the press, which he and his coalition of advisers carefully cultivated. Many journalists must have harbored an only barely suppressed wish to be part of the Kennedy gang, and thus forgave the young president everything: not only his heavy philandering, some of it upstairs in the White House, but the trivial facts that he smoked cigarettes and played golf (instructions to the press were that he was never to be photographed doing either). The complicated Bobby Kennedy–Marilyn Monroe nightmare was also suppressed until well after both parties were dead.

Much gossiping, and raking of muck, was done privately, and chiefly by people who hated the figures in question. Thus Franklin Roosevelt was said by his enemies to be both Jewish and homosexual. At a lower level of office than the presidency, gossip, if widely enough circulated, even if not picked up by the press, could stop a man's public career. Such was the case with Sumner Welles, rumors about whose homosexuality were so rampant that they forced Roosevelt to accept Welles's resignation as undersecretary of state and number-two man in the State Department. Welles was, it turned out, in fact gay.

Exposing the private lives of politicians in the press began in earnest with the advent of investigative journalism, which hit its height with the Watergate investigation, after which everything was fair game for exposure. Senator Gary Hart, thought to be a presidential candidate, fell early to the blade of investigative reporting when he was photographed aboard a yacht with a model on his lap. The FBI director J. Edgar Hoover, about whom rumors of transvestism abounded, was lucky to have died when he did, in 1972, just before open season was declared by the press — soon to be known as the media—on any human flaw or flagrancy that might create a stir. The stories about Hoover's being a cross-dresser remain one of the most wildly amusing of all modern gossip items.

Soon elected officials began falling like dandruff. Politicians known as bottom pinchers, heavy boozers, tax dodgers, and minor and major thieves were written up in the press and quickly thereafter written off. Their wives, too, were potential and real victims of the media gossip grinder. The scrutiny that any public figure is today expected to undergo, a kind of trial by media with public disgrace likely to follow, has meant that many capable people, unwilling to submit to such intense gossip and rumor mongering, steer clear of public office. Such is the indirect power and strong effect of gossip.

"The tone of politics," writes Gail Collins in *Scorpion Tongues: The Irresistible History of Gossip in American Politics,* from which I have acquired some of the material in this chapter, "had become more personal and more vicious." The advent of talk-radio shows, and more recently the Internet, further exacerbated things. Any notion of respect for the office of the presidency, or any other office, was now out the window. The Bill Clinton impeachment saga was more than sufficient evidence; so, too, stories about Hillary Clinton being a lesbian and simultaneously the lover of the Clinton aide Vincent Foster, who committed suicide. Lesbian, heterosexual adulterer—when it comes to gossip, all laws of contradiction are off the books.

"Most people who get their names in gossip columns," Roger Wilkes writes, "are there because they want to be." But is this true? Today one of the often unwanted side effects of celebrity is to leave one exposed as a target of gossip. In the 2009 U.S. Tennis Open, a determined seventeen-year-old girl named Melanie Oudin captured the fancy of the crowd by defeating a few seeded players on her way to (being defeated in) the quarterfinals, which brought her instant celebrity. Alas, it also brought out that her mother had had an affair with Melanie's coach, a matter that, stirred up in the swill of the tabloids, had to have caused much sadness to everyone in her family and drained away some of the pleasure of her triumphs on the court.

Living through others' lives is one of the chief attractions of celebrity gossip, which tends in some ways to be less malignant, because the personal motive is missing, than gossip about people one knows. With the advent of movies, which brought figures whose faces we could see up close, and then television, where the stars came (as the cliché has it) into our living rooms, everyone began to feel that once distant celebrities were more like family, or if not always like family, then better known to us than the quiet man who lives on the sixth floor. Richard Schickel captured this phenomenon in the title of his book *Intimate Strangers: The Culture of Celebrity in America*.

Up to roughly 1950, when television became an integral part of American domestic life, the number of national celebrities in the United States was distinctly limited: perhaps sixty or seventy of them were movie stars, another thirty or so were athletes, and perhaps twenty-five or so were national politicians.

At the national celebrity level, gossip itself tended to be more controlled, especially in Hollywood, the chief celebrity-making manufactory of the time. Yet some gossip-causing scandals were too large to be prevented: the Roscoe "Fatty" Arbuckle alleged rape and murder case in 1921 is a notorious example. But in the Hollywood of the 1930s and '40s, the two leading gossip columnists, Hedda Hopper and Louella Parsons, lived off the sufferance of the major studios, which parceled out tidbits to them, usually of a fairly mild kind: engagements, the pregnancies of stars or the wives of stars, the lending of one studio star to another studio for a special movie. Very little talk of drunkenness, adultery, homosexuality, or divorce was permitted. Stories did seep out—about Randolph Scott's alleged homosexuality, John Barrymore's boozing, Errol Flynn's sexual hijinks—but not by the means they do today: through the diligent work of the scavengers known as gossip columnists.

The great movie stars of the early Hollywood era were supposed to be just like the rest of us, but somehow luckier, because more gifted with talent and good looks, than the rest of us. Stories of monstrous behavior were out of bounds, while stories of their normality were encouraged. So we have the anodyne tales of movie stars coming from small towns (Ronald Reagan), being discovered at drugstore counters (Lana Turner), and other mythic beginnings of richly rewarded careers. We have Mickey Rooney playing Andy Hardy, that sweet, innocent kid down the street in small-town America, though the reality was that the late-adolescent Rooney chased every woman on the lot, and, to hear him tell it, caught quite a few. Once chosen, the movie star must not violate his mythic status as a normal human being by behavior thought abnormal. Charlie Chaplin, one of the few authentic geniuses in the history of Hollywood, violated this iron law of the normality of stars with his penchant for too young women and, later, his left-wing politics. When Gene Kelly's wife, Betsy Blair, who as a fellow traveler of the American Communist Party was in danger of exposure by the House Un-American Activities Committee, Kelly had no choice but to depart Hollywood and work for a number of years in Europe. Aberrations, political, sexual, or any other, were verboten.

Politicians may once again have regained preeminent standing in the creation of gossip. Today's Hollywood stars, rock musicians, and comedians no longer generate the intense interest that older movie stars did. This has to do with America no longer having the unified culture it once did. Up through the 1960s, a movie star or a popular singer tended to be a popular figure for the entire country, not just a segment of it, as is currently the case. Rock singers, for example, are of interest only to those who listen to rock. Bruce Springsteen may have an audience of several million fans, which is no small thing, but everyone was presumed to be interested in Frank Sinatra. The segmentation of mass culture — divided now by age, often by race, sometimes by geography — has divided up the national interest. Far from everyone cares about Madonna; no one failed to care about Marilyn Monroe. Not everyone knows who Will Smith is, no matter how grand the box office receipts of his movies; but it would have been difficult to find people who, when he was in his long prime, didn't know who Edward G. Robinson was. In the course of celebrity being divided in this way — ethnically, by age, by special interest — it has also become diluted.

Further dilution has occurred with the widening of celebrity through cable television, with its various soap operas, reality shows, and political chat shows. Liz Smith, perhaps the last of the old-line gossip columnists, not long ago remarked: "There aren't any big stars anymore. It's very diminished in quality, I guess is what I'd say, the quality of stardom. Because I don't know who most of these people are. I'm not kidding. I read Page Six [devoted to gossip in the *New York Post*] mystified every day, and everybody I talk to agrees with me. They don't know who anybody is."

Explaining this, the critic and editor John Podhoretz notes that the rise in gossip magazines and gossip television shows is partly responsible for this thinning out of celebrity. Lots more people are celebrated, but only for a short time: the current bachelor on the reality show *The Bachelor*, the professional dancer on *Dancing with the Stars*, the couple suspected of murdering their child, the plagiarist who flogged his book on *Oprah*, the male prostitute who turns in the not-out-of-the-closet state governor. Celebrities, each and all of them, famous for being famous, however briefly; but famous, too, because, as Podhoretz puts it, the organs of celebrity, print and electronic, need a continuing supply of names to "feed this inexhaustible maw." He adds that the "older methods of celebrity manufacture" — the Hollywood studios' public relations departments — "no longer suffice." With the old publicity machine of Hollywood inadequate to fill all the magazines and television shows (*Entertainment Tonight, Access Hollywood*, and the rest) devoted to celebrity, Podhoretz concludes, "celebrity and notoriety are indistinguishable, and the phenomenon of stardom, like so many American institutions, has been delegitimized."

Another component worth mentioning in all this is that the only way to large-scale celebrity today is through regular appearances on television or in movies or national politics. No matter your achievements, if you are not often seen doing what you do on the tube, or today possibly on YouTube, you may eventually acquire fame, but celebrity will elude you.

One of the great advantages that Hollywood celebrities of an earlier time had over those of the current day is that they didn't regularly appear on television talk shows to promote their films or their careers; this meant that they were excused from exposing their stupidities. Who today knows how smart or dopey James Cagney or Myrna Loy might have been? What can be known is that movie stars, and a great many others, gain in allure from our ignorance about them, for in the absence of any real knowledge we have, they are as smart and glamorous as we wish them to be.

A large part of the pleasure of contemporary gossip about celebrities has to do with that ugly little emotion that goes by the German word *Schadenfreude*, or pleasure in another's fall. Nice to think, is it not, that people gifted with good looks or acting ability or musical talent, rewarded for them with vast quantities of money, also have many of the problems that the rest of us might have, and often a few extra thrown in: children who didn't work out, struggles with diet, marital discord dragged out in public, bankruptcy, and so much more. If in some sense the cult of celebrity is about common people worshiping people luckier than themselves, owing to the good offices of gossip, a way has been found of evening the score, at least a little, by showing that in the end the very lucky often have it no better than we, and sometimes, thanks to the gods of fate and the merchants of gossip, it turns out that they have it even worse.

Diary

The playwright Lillian Hellman was sitting in a restaurant with a friend of mine when Arthur M. Schlesinger Jr., the historian and chronicler of the Kennedy family, walked in with his then new, much taller than he, wife. It seemed to be the season for men obsessed with politics to marry women much taller than themselves. (Henry Kissinger also married a woman much taller than he, and so did the columnist George F. Will.)

"There is Arthur with his new wife," Lillian said to my friend. "Extraordinary how much taller she is than he. Do you suppose Arthur goes up on her?"

GREAT GOSSIPS OF THE
WESTERN WORLD, II

The Bully

Grob, a Yiddish word meaning coarse, crude, rough, pushy, nicely describes the family into which Walter Winchell, for decades the most famous and perhaps most influential of all American journalists, was born. The family's original name was Weinschel, or Winschel, its city of origin Bialystok, in northeastern Poland near the border of what is now Belarus. Winchell's grandfather Chaim settled in America in 1881. He and his wife lived on the Lower East Side and raised a family of nine children. The firstborn, Jacob, was Winchell's father, but the second son, George, who acquired a seat on the New York Stock Exchange, was considered the head of the family in its second generation. Jacob was passed over because he was thought brash, a man of dubious taste, a bust-out, an embarrassment to his brothers and sisters who yearned for assimilated gentility. *Grob.*

Jacob's first child, Walter, was born, in 1897, into the black-sheep branch of his extended family, poor, with a father who never really gained a financial foothold and a mother who had no compunction about making her husband aware of her extreme disappointment in him. Jacob's philandering didn't ease matters. Extreme emotional instability and fear of poverty were the heavy pollutants of young Walter's life.

The result was that Walter Winchell, no matter how great his success in later years, tended permanently to view himself as an underdog, one of the insulted of the earth and a man always worried about money, though he earned a lot of it. Early in the game he decided that no one gives you anything for nothing, and that the world was divided between winners and losers, so a person had no choice but to scrap like mad to gain the upper hand in all things, little and large, and join the winners. Life, in Winchell's reading of it, was combat, full time, no holds barred.

The first move in Winchell's larger game plan was to get the hell out of his family's dreary home. He quit school at thirteen and left his family at the same time. Ernest Cuneo, who became a legal assistant to Mayor Fiorello La Guardia and later a power on the Democratic National Committee during the Franklin Delano Roosevelt years and who was a longtime friend of Winchell's—the last not an easy thing to do—claimed that his rough upbringing "had left him with four inches of scar tissue around his heart, and with a heart full of fear, [and] instead of some love, the fear of being broke."

Like many another of the New York Jewish kids of his generation who had no family business to fall back on, no interest in school or politics or culture, Winchell went into show business. He became a song plugger, then went onstage in vaudeville, as part of a trio that included a man named Jack Weiner, and George Jessel, later known as America's "toastmaster general" and a monumental bore of astounding self-importance.

Winchell's career as a song-and-dance man went onward but not all that far upward. He had the ambition, he had the energy—only the talent was missing. He worked the lesser vaudeville circuits. He teamed up with a young dancer named Rita Greene, whom he eventually married. A hoofer by trade, he was a hustler in spirit, and he hustled much better than he hoofed. He had also during these years discovered his true métier. He began, almost as a hobby, collecting gossipy items about vaudevillians, writing them up, then posting his typewritten sheets backstage, where people could discover who was making whoopie with whom and other intramural secrets about the interior wheelings and dealings of show biz. He had a newshound's sense of where to find fresh items—he was, that is to say, a natural snoop—and a genuine knack for turning these items into lively reading. Before long, Winchell would give up his tap shoes for tapping out tidbits on a typewriter.

Vaudeville, though, forged Walter Winchell, his spirit of competitiveness, his understanding that no greater sin exists than being dull in public. Neal Gabler, Winchell's excellent biographer, writes: "Vaudeville made Walter an entertainer for life and in life. Growing up in vaudeville as he did, he not only absorbed its diversity, its energy, its nihilism, and then deployed them in his journalism, but learned how to create his journalism *from* them: journalism as vaudeville." He understood journalism, in other words, to be essentially a form of entertainment.

Winchell's climb up the rickety rungs of journalism's ladder—working for *Vaudeville News, Billboard,* the health faddist Bernarr Macfadden's *New York Graphic,* eventually landing as the Broadway columnist on Joseph Medill Patterson's flagship paper, the *New York Daily News*—need not detain us. The important point is that Winchell made this climb through personal toughness and an impressive insensitivity to the feelings of everyone he wrote about or worked with. Jimmy Walker, when mayor of New York, told Winchell that "you can keep your friends and be a failure—or lose them and be a success." In Winchell's case this advice was easily heeded by a man who, in the most profound sense, was always in business solely for himself.

Winchell had a strong instinct for what caught the attention of the average man or woman. He invented a rat-a-tat prose style, punctuated by ellipses, laced with energetic slang, and sprinkled with neologisms of his own devising: booze in his columns became "giggle-water," mistresses "keptives," Broadway was "the Main Stem" or "Coffee Pot Canyon," "Chicagorilla" was a thug from the Second City, "apartache" stood for divorcing couples, and "Renovate" referred to a man or woman going off to Reno for a divorce, while couples expecting a child were "infanticipating."

Winchell's rise ran parallel with the rise of interest in personality in American journalism and in celebrity in the country at large—an interest that has only increased, if become more diffuse, in our own day. Winchell knew how to plumb this interest for all it could yield. Attacking large names was one of his specialties: early in his career he went after the Schubert brothers, then powerful satraps in Broadway theater. He also had an instinct for the weaknesses of the famous in New York, where fame could sometimes have the shelf life of cottage cheese, and where ever-fresh exposure to publicity, required by the constant stoking of a reputation, was required. "What can you get on the other fellow?" Winchell wrote. "What do you know about him? Is he doing something he'd be ashamed of, and how much is there in it for me?"

Operating on these principles—perhaps absence of principles is more like it—Walter Winchell himself became a celebrity, one of the noisiest in America. His column was soon widely syndicated, its author written up in *Editor and Publisher, Time, The New Yorker,* and elsewhere. His friend Ernest Cuneo said Winchell did for Broadway what Mark Twain did for the Mississippi—not true but doubtless nice to hear.

Although Winchell was considered very much a figure of the 1920s, the Depression that ushered in the '30s did not in the least slow him down. He switched his home base from the *Daily News* to Hearst's *New York Mirror,* and thence to the same publisher's *Journal,* which, along with his increased syndication, brought him an ever-wider readership. The Depression, which had the effect, as Neal Gabler points out, of dimming the lights on Broadway, at the same time widened the scope of Winchell's interests; he soon became, more than a mere Broadway gossip columnist, a journalist whose bailiwick was the entire country, his column carrying items on Hollywood, politics, and the international scene.

Winchell took a giant step when, in 1930, he took his gossip on the radio. His original show was on the air Monday nights from 7:45 to 8:00, featuring gossip items and an interview with an entertainment celebrity. Winchell made no bones about introducing himself as "New York's most notorious gossip," allowing that he has been called lots of other things, too. He was making a six-figure salary from his newspaper column along with a thousand dollars a program for his radio shows on WABC.

His radio audience grew to be larger than the already large audience for his newspaper column. He was now a star of the stature of the Irish tenor Morton Downey, Kate Smith, and Bing Crosby—all built on nothing more than purveying gossip. He was not above inserting himself into major criminal proceedings. Throughout the trial of Bruno Hauptmann, for the alleged kidnapping of the Lindbergh baby, he managed to call attention to himself in his columns and radio shows. At the capture of the criminal boss Louis "Lepke" Buchalter, he arranged to have Lepke turn himself in to him, Winchell, who brought him to the police. All this added greatly to his fame. One night a Broadway producer—drunk or not, it isn't known—asked, "Tell me, Winchell. What is going to happen to America if people like you are successful?" A good question, the answer to which is not yet in.

Winchell once said that the way to get famous is to throw a brick at someone who is already famous. People now began throwing bricks at him. Heywood Broun, a great name in journalism in the 1920s and '30s, claimed that Winchell's kind of gossip, everywhere invading privacy, was turning New York into a small town. "Who wants New York to have the same sort of underground wires which make small towns so mean and so petty?" Broun wrote. In the thirties, *The New Yorker* published a lengthy profile of Winchell by St. Clair McKelway (in 1940 this was molded into a book titled *Gossip: The Life and Times of Walter Winchell*), in which Winchell's inaccuracies were toted up, his political and criminal connections recounted, his sins in particular and in general catalogued. McKelway wrote:

There are men in New York who have been identified by Winchell, by means of crystal clear euphemisms, as homosexuals; there are people whose attempted suicides he has reported; there are married men and women who, in spite of Winchell's stated intention not to let his columns hurt happy marriages, have been linked with others of the opposite sex; there are couples whose separation has been reported when they were thinking of no such thing, whose impending marriage has been announced when it was not being considered by them; there are individuals whose affectionate regard for someone has been reported when they weren't sure of it themselves. Then, in the middle ground, there are people in New York whose professional aims have been misinterpreted or inaccurately reported; whose opinions have been garbled; whose anecdotes, not told in the presence of Winchell, have been ineptly retold by him, making them feel silly; whose appearances at night clubs have been made to seem more frequent than they really are. At the end of the list are people who merely object to having their names appear in Walter Winchell's column or in any gossip column under any circumstances.

None of this put the least dent in Winchell's shield. His column was published in more than 150 newspapers; a *Fortune* survey found him to be the most popular columnist in America. The opening of his fifteen-minute radio show, for which he was now getting paid $3,500 a shot, accompanied by a clacking telegraph sound—"Good evening, Mr. and Mrs. America and all the ships at sea"—was familiar to millions of Americans. Whether Winchell was a journalist or an entertainer was not a question that much bothered him. Neither did individual complaints about his having gone too far in one or another of his "items." "I wait until I can catch an ingrate with his fly open," Winchell wrote in his autobiography, "and then I take a picture of it." Oscar Levant remembered that whenever you complained to him about an item in his column, Winchell's response was "I'm a shitheel." He also said, "Democracy is where everybody can kick everybody else's ass. But you can't kick Winchell's."

By the late 1930s the brash gossip columnist's reputation and power—the two were of course linked—were of sufficient magnitude for President Roosevelt, who wanted Winchell on his side, to cultivate him. And successfully cultivate him FDR did; some said that Winchell, in his columns, became the president's unofficial spokesman, his link between the White House and the average American. He also became friendly with J. Edgar Hoover. Working the other side of the street, he had New York mob connections. Once, after Winchell was beaten up, he had bodyguards from both the FBI and Lucky Luciano's gang assigned to watch over him.

Through the early forties, Winchell was a great enemy of Hitler and thought of as a friend of the little man. At the same time, he was a chronicler of the rich and famous, noting their goings-on in such smart New York supper clubs as the Colony and El Morocco. He held personal court at the Stork Club, and his regular presence there was the making of that establishment and of its less than genial host, Sherman Billingsley. He acquired an all-wave radio for his car so he could listen to the police band and race to crime scenes at all hours.

With his easy arrogance and his power to break reputations and spoil lives, Winchell was a feared man. Arthur Brisbane, his editor at the *New York Mirror,* who didn't take to Winchell's throwing his weight around in the newsroom, once told him, "You have neither ethics, scruples, decency or conscience." To which Winchell replied, "Let others have those things. I've got readers." And he did; circulation figures climbed whenever he wrote for the paper. For Winchell life was a simple matter of power, and the person who had the most power dominated.

Meanwhile, he had become a great bore—"a thrilling bore," someone called him. "When he is not talking," St. Clair McKelway wrote, "he sits forward with his head raised unnaturally in an attitude of intense awareness. His heel is apt to beat quick time on the floor like a swing musician's, his gaze roves ceaselessly over the room, and his hands go on little fruitless expeditions over the tablecloth, up and down the lapels of his coat, in and out of his pockets." The playwright Clifford Odets wondered in his diary, after a night listening to Winchell gas away about himself at the Stork Club, "how a human being could have so little sense of other human beings."

He was also a bully, treating press agents, who were always eager to get their clients named in his column, with lofty, sometimes brutal, contempt. The 1957 movie *Sweet Smell of Success*, told in good part from the point of view of the press agent Sidney Falco (played brilliantly by Tony Curtis), is loosely based on Winchell's rough treatment of press agents, who were ready to do anything to ingratiate themselves with him. Meanwhile, Winchell treated kindly only those who had more power than he or those for whose services he had momentary need. Lord Acton wasn't quite right; it doesn't take absolute power to corrupt absolutely. Some people can arrive at the state of absolute corruption with a good deal less than absolute power, and Walter Winchell was one of them.

His career seemed endless in its upward sweep. He was on the cover of *Time* in the 1930s; at the end of the 1940s he was the highest-paid figure in show business. His column cleared the path for other gossip columnists: Leonard Lyons, Louis Sobol, Louella Parsons, Dorothy Kilgallen, Earl Wilson. Without Winchell, none of their columns would likely have come into existence.

One day in 1948, at a New York Yankees game, sitting with J. Edgar Hoover, Winchell mused on the possibility of running for president. He didn't have the same rapport with Harry Truman as he had had with Franklin Roosevelt. He took the side of General Douglas MacArthur against Truman in their controversy over Korea, which made him persona non grata at the White House. Once thought a liberal in politics, Winchell was, with the aid of Hoover's influence, much taken with Senator Joseph McCarthy; after all, as Neal Gabler suggests, their methods—accusations based on hearsay—were not all that different. Winchell became an anti-Communist of the disreputable kind that found Communists under every bed, and wasn't opposed to using smear tactics to ruin a man's reputation—an anti-Communist of the kind, in short, that gave sensible anti-Communism a bad name.

Hard to pinpoint the precise date when Walter Winchell's meteor began to descend. A racial incident at the Stork Club over seating the black dancer Josephine Baker, in which he did not truly have a part, but in which he defended his friend Sherman Billingsley who did, didn't help. A man named Lyle Stuart, who himself would go on to specialize in the scurrilous, wrote an attack on Winchell, claiming he did not write his own columns, that he had been having an affair with a showgirl, that he was an egomaniac capable of great viciousness, and that he was finally a sham. The *New York Post* also ran a series of articles attacking Winchell, emphasizing his journalistic inaccuracies, citing the careers he had helped destroy, claiming he had devised schemes to avoid paying his full share of income tax.

No work is a greater breeding ground than gossip for paranoia, into which Walter Winchell now submerged. In his case, he was a paranoid with real as well as imaginary enemies. Everywhere he had scores to settle. He started using his column and radio show to go after other radio commentators, fellow columnists, newspaper editors, and those suitors for his daughter of whom he didn't approve. He combined gossip and red-baiting, going after not merely the usual suspects but adding a few unusual ones, Adlai Stevenson notable among them. Always a man to keep bad company, he added Roy Cohn, McCarthy's then young henchman, to his roster of unattractive friends.

The slide began with the gradual cancellation of contracts, the reduction in workload. His ratings dropped; ABC, for whom he broadcast a television show, let him go. His newspaper employer, the Hearst Corporation, refused any longer to insure his column against libel. People who formerly would have lived in fear of his retribution now openly attacked him in public, as the society hostess Elsa Maxwell did on the *Jack Paar Show.* Paar would later call him "a silly old man"; which hurt more, the "silly" or the "old," would be difficult to say. *Sweet Smell of Success,* taken from a story by a former press agent, Ernest Lehman, and with everyone assuming that the part of the out-and-out-bastard columnist was Walter Winchell, turned out to be an enormous hit — it also happens to be a swell movie — though Winchell tried to kill it in his column by claiming it was a financial dud.

The 1960s saw Winchell out. He began picking the wrong

horses in politics, claiming, for example, that John F. Kennedy was a Communist sympathizer. The Stork Club went belly-up. Hedda Hopper and Louella Parsons were done for in Hollywood, their services no longer required now that the studio system was ending. Winchell lost his column when his most recent home base, Hearst's *World Journal Tribune,* closed down in 1967. In a piece marking the end of Winchell's column, a writer on the *New York Times* noted that the column ended because of the "rise of television, a growing sophistication among newspaper readers, the decline of Hollywood and the emergence of an international set of performers who no longer read or care about Broadway and show business columns, changes in reading taste, a growing uneasiness about the truth of many [of his] column items and even changing sexual mores." Winchell had given a certain tone to an era—brash, intensely urban, tough-guy—but that era was finished, and so was he.

Walter Winchell without a column was like Babe Ruth without a bat, Jascha Heifetz without a violin, Mae West without a bosom. Little succor was to be found for him in a retreat into family life. He had long before alienated his daughter Walda. His son, Walter Winchell Jr., never able to find a place in life, committed suicide at the age of thirty-three. Winchell himself died two months before reaching seventy-five, and fifteen days after the death of his wife.

Winchell, Neal Gabler notes, simultaneously enlivened and vulgarized journalism. He advanced the spread of gossip, not merely individual items but the thing itself, throughout American newspapers, infecting so-called straight news with it, and making what were once back-alley whisper stories into front-page news. He whetted and fed the appetite for scandal about celebrities. He was in some sense the founding father of all the celebrity gossip magazines and television shows that now deluge our culture.

In Gabler's words, Winchell's legacy was to cause us to "believe in our entitlement to know everything about our public figures. We would believe that fame is an exalted state but suspect that the famous always have something to hide. Above all, we would believe in a culture of gossip and celebrity where entertainment takes primacy over every other value."

Would all this have happened anyway, even if Winchell had not lived? Maybe, maybe not. But in him man and subject were perfectly joined. His need for recognition, his disregard for the feelings of others, his shrewd sense of self-promotion, his tireless pursuit of the scandalous—all this made Walter Winchell the gossip columnist par excellence, which is perhaps the most dubious possible compliment a journalist can be paid.

Diary

An interview with Orson Welles is no small thing, and the journalist showed up at an expensive restaurant for a latish lunch in Los Angeles to discover that Welles had preceded him and was already seated. They tucked into a very grand lunch. No surprise, this, for Orson Welles was, to speak euphemistically, a substantial man; to speak uneuphemistically, he weighed more than three hundred pounds. The interview went well. The meal was a full one: drinks, starters, soup, large main courses, two bottles of wine, heavy desserts, cognac and coffee. At the conclusion of lunch and interview, Welles announced he must be on his way. The journalist thanked him, he hoped not too obsequiously. With Welles now departed, he asked for the check. He expected it to be large, but when it arrived he was flabbergasted. He also couldn't decipher how it had risen to this stratospheric sum. He called the waiter over to ask for an explanation.

"You see, sir," said the waiter, "Mr. Welles arrived something like an hour and a half ahead of you, and had a full lunch before you showed up. He instructed us to put it on your check."

12

Antediluvian Gossip

*I never travel without my diary. One should always have some-
thing sensational to read on the train.*

— GWENDOLYN FAIRFAX IN *The Importance of Being Earnest*

IN HER NOVEL *Daniel Deronda* George Eliot called gossip "a
sort of smoke that comes from the dirty tobacco pipes of
those who diffuse it; it proves nothing but the bad taste of
the smoker." True enough, but as an astonishingly smart woman
and a great novelist, Eliot also knew how central gossip could be
not only to moving forward dramatic action in novels but to alter-
ing life itself. The latter knowledge she came by at first hand. In
1854 Eliot (née Mary Ann Evans) entered into a union with G. H.
Lewes, a married man who, owing to complex English law, could
not be legally divorced from his first wife. Because of her unconventional partnership, Eliot's social life was less than comfortable;
she was often the victim of gossip of the meanest kind, with the
consequence that she did not go much, and probably never light-
heartedly, into society.

A minor character in *Daniel Deronda*, a Mr. Vandernoodt, reporting a pertinent piece of gossip to Daniel, the novel's eponymous hero, remarks that "there are plenty of people who knew
all about it"—the secret family of the man whom the heroine

of the novel is to marry—"but such stories get packed away like old letters. They interest me. I like to know the manners of my time—contemporary gossip, not antediluvian." The distinction between contemporary and antediluvian gossip is a useful one, especially when it comes to public gossip, or gossip about celebrity figures.

As for contemporary gossip, at some point age kicks in and one loses interest in the people around whom gossip of the day swirls most vigorously. Long ago it kicked in for me. I don't regularly read any gossip column. I sometimes check the *New York Post*'s Page Six, though I am lucky if on any given day I know half the subjects of its gossip items; even when I know of them, usually vaguely, I find myself a good deal less than excited by the revelations about them. That a rock singer trashed a luxurious hotel room and left dirty needles and used feminine-hygiene products behind, "according to sources," and also flooded the floor, doesn't arouse much interest in me. Nor does the indecent proposal that a movie star made years ago to a 1960s model at a Hollywood party light my fire. As for Todd Phillips, Brian Grazer, Chosan Nyugen, Mary J. Blige, Michael Hirtenstein, Ed "Jean Luc" Kleefield, Cydney Bernard, Tara Subkoff, Rikki Klieman, and Count Alex de Lesseps, names that all appeared on Page Six on a recent day, I can only ask, in the words of the Sundance Kid to his friend Butch, "Who are these guys?"

I don't currently watch any of the television shows dedicated to gossip about movie and television stars. I don't watch the soaps, and I watch no so-called reality TV, both of which, in a gossip-drenched time, provide low-grade celebrity subjects for contemporary gossip. I realize that there are now celebrity chefs and celebrity dermatologists to the stars, and I have even seen a reference to a celebrity gardener in the Hamptons, but I am not displeased at my inability to call up any of their names. While standing in the supermarket checkout line, I glimpse the grocery press—the *National Enquirer,* the *Globe,* and the rest—but increasingly I am mystified about the subjects of the stories that appear there. When not mystified, I cannot bring myself to care, certainly not about that lead-dust triangle of Angelina Jolie, Brad Pitt, and Jennifer Aniston, about the poundage freshly arriving and slowly departing from the carcass of Oprah Winfrey, about the child adoption problems of Madonna, about the lowjinks of Paris Hilton, and about the goings-on of lesser mortals. When I see a magazine cover whose headline is "Jake's Web of Lies," and another with "What Ali's Hiding," I haven't a clue about who Jake and Ali might be, and find I cannot stir myself sufficiently to care. As I write, the marital meltdown of a couple named Jon and Kate Gosselin—they have a reality television show, I learned, called *Jon and Kate Plus 8*—is getting a great amount of publicity in the grocery gutter press, but my own fond expectation is that, by the time this book is published, their names will be deep down in the crowded dustbin of gossip history.

Much gossip that continues to be purveyed now qualifies as quasi-, or perhaps semi-, antediluvian, in Mr. Vandernoodt's term. This includes gossip about these hardy perennials of modern but no longer contemporary figures: various members of the Kennedy family, the British royals, the artful (now dead) dodgers Richard Nixon and Lyndon Johnson, Marilyn Monroe, Elvis, Princess Diana, O. J. Simpson. Hardy perennials, after all, they remain hardy and perennial. A story not long ago emerged about Marlon Brando having slept on two different occasions with Jackie Onassis. The story derives from a book that also has Mrs. Onassis canoodling with her brother-in-law Bobby. *Wunderbar!*

My own taste in gossip, unlike Mr. Vandernoodt's, tends to run to the antediluvian, but it tends also to run to the highbrow. Either you care about Rosie O'Donnell or you don't. I don't, not in the least. I prefer my gossip analytical and refined. I care a lot less for gossip about Conan O'Brien than I do for gossip about Conor Cruise O'Brien. I cannot bring myself to become faintly interested in even the most lurid stories of the latest passing celebrity schlepper ("Celebrity Butcher Found Dead in Freezer"). But when I read, as I not long ago did in the *Times Literary Supplement*, that two of Cary Grant's (five) wives alleged physical abuse on his part, it gets my attention, though Grant is long gone. It does so because Grant was an immensely attractive figure; though an actor, not a notably cerebral profession, he appears to have had a thought or two of some originality. ("I pretended to be somebody I wanted to be until finally I became that person. Or he became me," he said of his charming screen persona.) Why would a man so gifted by the gods and privileged by the world as Cary Grant—with good looks, money, fame—feel the need to beat up women? Something worth contemplating here: gossip, in other words, as food for thought.

I am only interested in gossip about people whom I find intrinsically interesting. Often, as with Cary Grant, these turn out to be dead people, some dead for quite a long while. In a recent reading of *Pages from the Goncourt Journals,* for example, I was pleased to hear the long-ago gossip that Guy de Maupassant was the illegitimate son of Gustave Flaubert; that Talleyrand may have been the father of the painter Eugène Delacroix; that Émile Zola probably had an enlarged prostate, causing him to piddle frequently on short train trips; that the food at the home of Princess Mathilde Bonaparte was wretched; that the Comte de Montesquiou, Proust's model for Baron de Charlus, had a love affair with a female ventriloquist who, "while Montesquiou was straining to achieve his climax, would imitate the drunk voice of a pimp, threatening the aristocratic client." Now that's what I call quality gossip, antediluvian though it assuredly is.

The hunger for gossip feeds much modern biography. Of a biography of Somerset Maugham, a reviewer in the *Times Literary Supplement* (October 9, 2008) writes: "What reads like a thoroughly traditional, archive-based cradle-to-grave biography in fact includes a good deal of gossip and speculation." But the same hunger for gossip, for the inside, unofficial, and true story, can still attach to long-deceased subjects of biography. The first successful modern biography was James Boswell's *Life of Johnson,* though some say Samuel Johnson himself wrote the first modern biographies in his *Lives of the Poets.* Boswell, readers of the day must have thought, had given them the real lowdown on the great man, recounting anecdotes about him, eliciting his opinions, whenever possible allowing him to speak for himself. But the lowdown would in time get much lower still, lower than lots of people might wish to go. In a review of two recent biographies of Johnson, Pat Rogers, a scholar of eighteenth-century literature, provides this arresting paragraph:

> One issue which has provoked a great deal of discussion is Johnson's possible taste for masochistic sex. This derives from a padlock left with Hester Thrale and some suspicious references to chains and punishment (some in a letter coded in French that he wrote to Hester). Martin [Peter Martin, the author of one of the biographies under review] states baldly that the suggestion, originally made by the scholar Katherine Balderston, "has been discredited." The rashness of this claim emerges when we turn to Meyers [Jeffrey Meyers, the author of the second biography], who supports the prosecution case with a quote from Krafft-Ebing. Personally, I am with Meyers on this, but the facts are not conclusive, and, though biographers have to make up their mind on such points, it is only fair to the reader if they admit the scale of disagreement. Similarly Meyers buys easily into the theory that a mysterious letter M which crops up in Samuel's journal reveals "a painful and unceasing struggle with masturbation." As Martin shows, there are other and maybe more plausible explanations, notably a record of bowel movements.

After reading this passage, one would prefer to be a Baptist minister in a small town who has been found dead drunk on Sunday morning on the steps of his church than a great critic and man of letters whose private life is exposed to the speculations of modern scholars centuries after his death. Not a pretty thing to have academics argue that you—as in the case of Samuel Johnson, an earnest Christian and in his generosity to the downtrodden a genuinely saintly man—are into masochistic sex and that you have had a lifelong problem with masturbation. Yet under the banner of scholarship this sort of loose, gossipy talk goes on all the time, and often its targets are precisely the people who would find it most appalling.

For many years now, scholars and critics have been earnestly at work on what I think of as the HJHP, or Henry James Homosexual Project. Although there is no evidence that Henry James ever made actual physical love to anyone, woman or man, biographers have been keen to prove that his abstinence has hid James's true sexual nature, which many of them feel was homosexual. Such evidence as has been adduced on behalf of this gossipy speculation is that James, late in life, wrote effusive letters to a sculptor named Hendrik Andersen and other younger men, and also that he became a great hugger of men. Thin stuff, one would have thought: as for the letters, James had long been an epistolary master of what he himself called "mere gracious twaddle," which entailed deliberately, even comically overstated effusions; as for the hugging, if hugging a man is a sign of homosexuality, then there goes Hollywood and the entire National Basketball Association, where the hug between men long ago replaced the handshake. One of James's biographers has him sharing a night in the same bed, when young, with his contemporary Oliver Wendell Holmes Jr., and the novelist Colm Tóibín used this scene in a novel, *The Master*, that argues the case for James's homosexuality. Scholars have also found that Abraham Lincoln, when young, shared a bed for a few nights with another man, with findings similar to those against Henry James. Biographers tend to prefer the flashier explanation of latent or overt homosexuality over that of a simple shortage of beds in the nineteenth century: the young Abe Lincoln was poor; Holmes and James were on a camping party when sharing their bed.

Why would those who have an intellectual investment in Henry James's homosexuality feel the need to make their case? Some are themselves homosexual, and perhaps it gives them a spiritual boost to have another great writer turn out also to be homosexual. Others who are not themselves homosexual perhaps wish to appear on the edge of discovery. In any case, the HJHP, with its pretense to scholarship, is very much in the gossipy spirit of the times.

Behind the HJHP and so much pathographical biography is

the advent and spread of Freudianism. Freud's major notions have by now been largely disqualified: the Oedipus complex, penis envy, the absolute importance of the first few years of a child's upbringing, the centrality of sex as the motor force of human life, the need to release repression, and the rest of it. But what hasn't disappeared, and perhaps never will, is the unspoken but patently apparent Freudian notion that we all have something to hide, and, corollarily, that which we are hiding is likely to be the most important thing about us. Freudianism, though its founder may not have intended it, has been a great goad to gossip.

Come to think of it, aren't the assumptions behind gossip similar to those behind Freud's? Everyone has something to hide—like as not, something very important—and it is gossip's job, like Freudian psychotherapy's, to ferret it out and spread it around; to be sure, for purposes of damnation, titillation, or simple entertainment rather than the melioration of suffering, as Freud wished. But not only do Freudians, literary biographers, and gossips tend to believe that the truth is hidden; so pervasive is the notion, we almost all do. "I found myself," the Oxford wit Maurice Bowra wrote to a friend after traveling in Italy, "a horrible discovery. I have been trying to lose myself ever since."

Every memoirist, autobiographer, and interesting letter writer presumes to report that he has something to tell us that is hidden. Like a good gossip, all are committed to indiscretion. In the twenty-first century, it has become fashionable to write memoirs about one's own addiction, incest, abuse, and madness. Memoirs have also begun to be used to pay back parents or husbands or wives, featuring their egregious mistreatment of the memoirist. Might telling such stories about oneself be the last refuge, or perhaps the first defense, not of the scoundrel but of the gossip?

Gay Talese, the author of *Thy Neighbor's Wife*, an investigative journalist's account of the sexual revolution, is currently writing a book about his marriage. The interest in his marriage, one gathers, has to do with how and why his wife, a woman better born socially than he and of some reputation in New York publishing, allowed her husband so many liberties in order to research his book, which required him to hang around public baths, massage parlors, orgy rendezvous, bordellos, and other steamy venues. The question, one gathers, is going to be How did the Talese marriage survive the husband's research? Perhaps in this new book Talese will reveal his love affairs, and perhaps he will reveal his wife's (if any) love affairs. The reigning assumption behind the book, though, is the dubious one that lots of people care.

The slick magazines love such material, and have for some while. As long ago as the early 1970s, a friend of mine was taken to lunch by an editor of *Esquire* to discuss the possibility of his writing an article on Robert Lowell. "How thoroughly ought I to go into Lowell's poetry?" my friend, no naïf, asked after his second glass of wine. "Oh," said the editor, "not all that thoroughly. I suspect the readers of *Esquire* have a good knowledge of Lowell's poetry already in hand." What *Esquire* wanted, of course, was the dish on Robert Lowell's many nervous breakdowns—he was manic-depressive—and his extramarital affairs during his manic swings. My friend suggested another bottle of wine.

He never wrote the article, and it was just as well, for Lowell pretty much did the job himself, on himself, in his poetry. In a book called *The Dolphin* (1973), Lowell wrote a series of not very good sonnets in which he recounts his breakdowns (*"The hospital. My twentieth in twenty years . . ."*), quoting letters from the wife he deserted (Elizabeth Hardwick), dragging his then thirteen-year-old daughter and the effect of his desertion on her into it all, and setting out some of the details of his life with a new wife (the Guinness brewery heiress Lady Caroline Blackwood). Such self-gossip, aired in public print, doesn't leave much for the professional gossips.

What Robert Lowell wrote became known as confessional poetry—among others strong in this line have been John Berryman, Sylvia Plath, Anne Sexton, and scores of younger, lesser practitioners—which gave self-gossiping the imprimatur of art. But this habit of nonreligious confession has long since spread further.

Only the other day I received an e-mail from a younger writer telling me that I wrote something too critical of a deceased novelist who was kind to him when he, the younger writer, suffered a manic crash from his bipolar disease. As part of the e-mail, he included an account of one of his manic episodes, which he apparently delivered before an audience. Now why should I need to know that this man, who has no connection with me, has this sad illness? What makes him so pleased to let me know about it—a pleasure tantamount to that which, in another day, some vicious gossip might have found in telling me of it? Very strange, all of it, and all but officially part of our culture.

I prefer the time when well-told gossip was itself an art, not a sloppy confession told out of the confessional box (a different spin on the phrase "thinking outside the box"). Gossip as pure art form is handsomely on display in *Letters from Oxford,* the letters being those that then young historian Hugh Trevor-Roper wrote to entertain the much older art connoisseur Bernard Berenson, pocketed away at I Tatti, his opulent Florentine villa, where he held court for an unending round of distinguished visitors. "Now all this is gossip," Trevor-Roper writes early in their correspondence, "and you know that I (like Logan)"—Pearsall Smith, Berenson's brother-in-law—"hate gossip." He is of course being ironic; Logan Pearsall Smith himself said, "Hearts that are delicate and kind and tongues that are neither—these make the best company." Later Trevor-Roper asks, "Now what new indiscretions can I offer you?" A bit further on he writes, "But I see that I am getting (as I easily do) malicious. I must stop at once, before I exhibit the worst side of my character."

Trevor-Roper deals chiefly in intellectual gossip, which is what old Berenson wants to hear. He informs him that Lewis Namier, who is, in his opinion, "the greatest living historian writing in English," is also, "without doubt, the greatest living bore. And for that distinction the competition, I'm afraid, is even hotter." Trevor-Roper compares Maurice Bowra, the warden of Wadham College, to Long John Silver and notes that he "boomed out of existence all conversation but his own." (Meanwhile, one learns from a recent biography of Bowra that in a letter to Evelyn Waugh he pronounced Trevor-Roper "a fearful man, short-sighted, with dripping eyes, shows off all the time, sucks up to me, boasts, is far from poor owing to his awful book [*The Last Days of Hitler*], on every page of which there is a howler.")

When the actor John Gielgud is caught propositioning a young man in a public bathroom, Trevor-Roper announces "the *jihad*" that respectable English society is on against homosexuals, remarking that "now, I am told, in the panic fear which has swept through the brotherhood [of homosexuals] the plainest of women are finding themselves in great demand, feminine company being, in society, the only protection against grave imputations." He writes of the social and intellectual climbing of the publisher George Weidenfeld, "whose social ascent still continues: having graduated from the world of journalism to the world of literature, he has now risen (according to some standards of hypsometry) still higher, and from literary duchesses has ascended to the world of pure duchesses, duchesses who, so far from even dabbling in literary fashions, are totally illiterate."

Gossip is here played as a grand game. And so Trevor-Roper fills Berenson in on Oxford intramural battles over appointments, elections, reputations. When he has run out of such gossip, which is never for long, Trevor-Roper writes apologetically to Berenson that "we shall have to confine new conversation, *faute de mieux,* to the Good, the True and the Beautiful." Berenson's enjoyment of young Trevor-Roper's gossip did not stop him from taking the latter's own measure in his diary, describing the historian as "cocksure, arrogant, but without insolence . . . Seldom starts, but when cranked up goes on endlessly with infinite detail, and detective awareness and marvelous capacity for taking trouble to convince himself and to convince his hearers . . . A fascinating letter-writer, indeed an epistolary artist, brilliant reviewer of all sort of books, very serious historian and formidable polemicist."

The need to take the measure of people, a trait of the British intellectual of a certain day, seems naturally to issue in gossip. "Life is not worth living," the political philosopher Isaiah Berlin wrote, "unless one can be indiscreet to intimate friends." In an interview with his biographer, Berlin noted: "I have a natural tendency to gossip, to describing things, to noticing things, to interest in human beings and their characters, to interplay between human beings, which is completely independent of my intellectual pursuits."

This interest in human character, leading naturally to gossip, is connected with the English appetite for bringing people down a peg, which adds a piquant touch of malice to the proceedings. In the hands of a gossip artist, with comic genius at his service, such as the novelist Evelyn Waugh, one gets gossip that is art deftly mixed with pure malice. When told that Randolph Churchill, the raucous son of Winston Churchill, went into the hospital for a tumor that turned out to be benign, Waugh told people that "the one thing about Randolph that isn't malignant and they removed it." Or, in a letter to his friend Nancy Mitford, he reports that Graham Greene, sitting in a hotel lobby in New York, discovered blood pouring from his penis and fainted. "'Well [the doctors reported to him], we can't find anything wrong at all. What have you been up to? Too much womanizing?' 'No, not for weeks since I left my home in England' [Greene replied]. 'Ah,' they said, '*that's* it.' What a terrible warning. No wonder his books are sad."

Nancy Mitford, Waugh's friend and correspondent, gave as good as she got, reporting that the literary critic Cyril Connolly caught his two mistresses cheating on him and said, almost in tears, "It *is* hard, here I have been absolutely faithful to 2 women for a year, they've both been unfaithful to me." Gossip among such people was an entertainment, and hence a gift, best wrapped in amusing language. And it is of course even better when it seems disinterested, devoid of personal ill will, told for the pure delight it brings to its auditors.

Nothing nowadays quite exists on the Trevor-Roper/Waugh/ Mitford level of gossip as an art form. One has to go to older books to find it, the way diehard moviegoers, unable to take deep pleasure in current movies, have to live off the swell movies of the past.

Diary

Two sophisticated women meet on the corner of Seventy-ninth Street and Madison Avenue in Manhattan. One reports to the other that she has heard gossip that the *New York Post* columnist Max Lerner is soon to marry the still young, still ravishing Elizabeth Taylor. Since Lerner is far from comely, and his writings are crushingly boring in a way that suggests their author must be also, the second woman asks, "Are you sure about this?" The first woman replies that it comes from a very reliable source. "My Lord, Elizabeth Taylor and Max Lerner," says the second woman. "Well, I guess I'd rather fuck him than read him." Which has always seemed to me the most devastating criticism of an author I have ever heard.

13

Literary Gossip

Go to a gossip's feast, and go with me:
After so long grief, such festivity.

— SHAKESPEARE, *The Comedy of Errors*

MARCEL PROUST AND his beloved mother, when gossiping together, which they did frequently, used to refer to "the full biography" when talking about people they knew. The full biography meant the real story, the reality behind the appearance, the true dish, the richest gossip. Proust's appetite for personal details, conveyed with the greatest precision, was unslakable. He loved gossip in and for itself, but he also had a professional interest in it, for he was a novelist, the greatest novelist of the twentieth century, and he understood that gossip and the novel were inextricable, that gossip undergirds almost all novels.

Many novels turn on gossip—that is, on characters in the novels finding out things that they are not supposed to know about other characters' secrets, hidden opinions, hitherto unknown motivations. This information causes blinders to fall away, so that insights result, with the consequence that some characters grow wiser, and narratives march off in unexpected directions, making it possible for novels, or at least the better ones, to come to unpredictable though plausible conclusions.

Each of Jane Austen's six novels, set as they are mainly in small-ish English towns, pivots on some crucial piece of gossip that, once revealed, changes the action of the novel decisively. "Indeed, Mrs. Smith, we must not expect to get real information from such a line [from gossip, that is]," exclaims Anne Elliot, the heroine of Austen's *Persuasion*. "Facts or opinions which are to pass through the hands of so many, to be misconceived by folly in one, and ignorance in another, can hardly have much truth left." Although some say that the character of Anne speaks as much as any of her characters for the author herself, my advice is not to believe what I have just quoted Anne Elliot saying. Even when gossip is mistaken, its importance cannot be gainsaid, and Jane Austen knew it. The same Mrs. Smith reports to Anne: "Call it gossip if you will; but when nurse Rooke has half an hour's leisure to bestow on me, she is sure to have something to relate that is entertaining and profitable, something that makes one know one's species better. One likes to hear what is going on, to be *au fait* as to the newest modes of being trifling and silly. To me, who lives so much alone, her conversation I assure you is a treat." Now that sounds closer to Austen's true view of gossip. And in *Persuasion* it is just such a bit of information, which begins in gossip but turns out to be truth, that resolves the complication of all that has gone before in the novel.

Elizabeth Gaskell, the Brontës, Edith Wharton, and Henry James, novelists who had a strong interest in gossip and made good use of it in their fiction, understood both gossip's attractions and its literary value. So, too, did writers whom one doesn't think of as primarily social novelists. Gossip plays a strong hand in *War and Peace* and *Anna Karenina*, as it does in the novels of Balzac, Dickens, and Flaubert. A critic named Homer Obed Brown has gone so far as to say that "it is probable that part of the pleasure we derive from the classic novel is a pleasure similar to that derived from gossip." Speculation on character, curiosity about other worlds, an interest in social status, the unveiling of secrets, nice discriminations, revelations of hidden motivations, moral judgments—so many of the constituent parts of gossip are also often at play in novels. One difference, of course, is that novels sometimes have didactic purposes, but then, who is to say that sometimes gossip mightn't, too?

Like gossips, writers of fiction do not always entirely make things up, at least most of the time they don't. Science fiction, horror tales, romances, detective stories, fantasies, and a few other genres may be almost wholly imagined, but much serious fiction is drawn from life—sometimes from actual events, ofttimes using actual people as life models on whom to create fictional characters.

As a writer of stories, I prefer to invent characters and situations, and often do. But perhaps just as often I have borrowed my stories from events that have taken place in my life, or that I have heard about, and draw characters from acquaintances or people about whom I have heard extraordinary or touching or frightful things. I try to disguise my characters' origins in so-called real life—some I disguise more carefully than others—and sometimes put someone I know through a series of incidents that I know have been undergone by someone else. I have written stories in which only one character is based, however roughly, on someone I have known, while every other, along with the plot of the story, are wholly the work of the imagination. Or I will give an invented character the occupation of someone I know only slightly. Not uncommonly readers have told me that they recognize characters in one or another of my stories; and more often than not, they are wrong. At such times, I try to let them down gently, because when they think they recognize a character as someone they know or have known, they feel a pleasure in it, as if they have broken a code, or, better still, been let in on a juicy bit of gossip.

Many writers of fiction do not go for the minimum disguise of their characters. Saul Bellow seems not to have invented many characters, only to have invented sins to give to characters who, for those in the know, have real-life analogues. Connoisseurs of his novels can point out that this woman was a girlfriend of the author's at Tuley High School, that lawyer botched Bellow's third divorce, this misery of a woman was one of his wives. Bellow was a literary Bluebeard, murdering his former wives not in life but in his fiction, and doing so without mercy. He regularly used his fiction to settle old scores. In his last novel, *Ravelstein,* he has his main character say of another character, who happens to have been a friend of mine, that he was homosexual and smelled bad. Both items are utterly false, but Bellow was repaying my friend for what he took to be many slights when he was still alive. Under the cover of fiction, this is gossip with the clear motive of vengeance behind it.

Biographers and critics of Proust eagerly point out that this character is based on Mme. Georges Aubernon, that on Robert de Montesquiou, another on Comte Henry Greffulhe. The supposition is that in reading about Proust's characters drawn from life we also learn about their life models. Sometimes we do, but sometimes not, as Proust transmogrifies certain of the models on which his characters are based, and sometimes, for his own good artistic reasons, does the reverse, making them less monstrous than they might actually have been in life.

Then, of course, there are the straight romans à clef, or (literally) novels with a key, which are only very thinly disguised portraits from life, meant to fool no one, with knowledge of the real-life characters supplying the key. Whenever the spirit of roman à clef is at work in fiction, the all but irresistible temptation is to extrapolate from the book back into life. The pleasure is in feeling that one is getting the real inside view of famous people, truth that cannot be spoken except through the veil of fiction—a purely gossipy pleasure.

Often such fiction serves as scarcely more than a legal prophylactic against libel. The first roman à clef I encountered as a younger reader was Simone de Beauvoir's *The Mandarins,* a novel based on the French existentialists of the 1940s, including most notably Jean-Paul Sartre, de Beauvoir herself, and Albert Camus, and others. The Chicago novelist Nelson Algren, with whom de Beauvoir had an affair on a visit she made to America, also appears, all too transparently, in *The Mandarins,* a fact that Algren came to view as little more than an embarrassment and a nuisance, suggesting on more than one occasion that the affair seemed to mean a lot more to Mlle. de Beauvoir than it did to him. E. I. Lonoff, the key figure in Philip Roth's novel *The Ghost Writer*, is everywhere taken to be the novelist Bernard Malamud—so much so that a recent biographer of Malamud's takes it to be a life drawing, even though much else in the novel is invention. E. L. Doctorow's *Book of Daniel* is about the children of Julius and Ethel Rosenberg, who were executed for spying for the Soviet Union. In this instance, the obvious roman à clef permits the novelist to make his case for what he feels: the injustice and terrible human consequences of the execution.

The possibilities for mischief here are considerable. Being portrayed as a vile character in someone's novel cannot be a pleasant experience. Impotent anger must be the result if one is portrayed as villainous, mild distaste even if one is portrayed favorably yet vulgarly. Isaiah Berlin was apparently used as a model for the central character in a series of detective stories by the writer Jocelyn Davey (the pseudonym for Chaim Raphael), which much put him off. "To appear in a novel of this kind," Berlin wrote to a colleague, "is rather like appearing in other people's dreams: and one cannot exactly avoid doing so, nor is one responsible for the shape one takes, and yet the results inevitably offend one. I wish people left one alone." But people won't leave one alone, especially if one is famous, even mildly so—at least they won't in the new era of widening gossip.

Soon enough the *roman* was dropped, making the *clef* unnecessary, and in the late 1960s a group of writers began to employ the techniques of fiction to write about famous people in a novelistic way under their true names, usually to their detriment. The enterprise was called the New Journalism, and though it is now far from new, and hasn't, truth be told, worn all that well, the phenomenon greatly lowered the bar on privacy and what it was permissible to say about people in print.

One of the most famous early pieces of the New Journalism

is Gay Talese's *Esquire* article "Frank Sinatra Has a Cold" (1966). Immensely readable, it gives the feeling that one is a privileged member of Sinatra's entourage. Talese is careful to show the deep contradictions in Sinatra, his generosity and his cruelty, his loyalty and how easily he slips into the role of bully. One assumed Sinatra was a monster, but after reading the article one feels certain he was. My guess is that what probably most excited readers of the article is the bits of gossip that arise out of it: Sinatra's manner with women, his twenty-six hairpieces (and the then impressive $400-a-week salary he paid a woman to tend them, toting them around in attaché cases), the Mafia don–like relations he has with so many people who seem to fear and revere him in roughly though not quite equal parts, his relations with his ex-wives and other women. All this is the stuff of good gossip, and the chief impression the article conveys—and this may have been the reigning virtue of the New Journalism generally—is that it was purveying the behind-the-scenes truth about real lives, which is of course what gossip claims for itself.

Another early specimen of the New Journalism is an article that the movie critic Rex Reed wrote on Ava Gardner (also in *Esquire,* in 1968), just as the beautiful movie star's career had begun its slide. In the piece Reed seems to be just hanging out with Miss Gardner, to have earned her trust, which he will soon enough betray by writing about her in a gossip-feeding way. He records the extent of her drinking, which is prodigious, and her sense of her own failure as an actress, which is sad. Here is a sample paragraph:

> She rolls her sleeves higher than the elbows and pours two more champagne glasses full [one with cognac, the other with Dom Pérignon]. There is nothing about the way she looks, up close, to suggest the life she has led: press conferences accompanied by dim lights and an orchestra; bullfighters writing poems about her in the press; rubbing Vaseline between her bosoms to emphasize the cleavage; roaming restlessly around Europe like a woman without a country, a Pandora with her suitcases

full of cognac and Hershey bars ("for quick energy"). None of the ravaged, ruinous grape-colored lines to suggest the affairs or the brawls that bring the police in the middle of the night or the dancing on tabletops in Madrid cellars till dawn.

Reed has caught Ava Gardner drunk—later in the evening she will down three iced tea–size glasses of tequila, hold the salt—which gives him an opening to ask her about her famous husbands: Mickey Rooney, Artie Shaw, and Frank Sinatra. When he mentions Sinatra's marriage to Mia Farrow, she laughs: "Hah, I always knew Frank would end up in bed with a boy." She allows that her accomplishments as an actress have been pitiful: "Hell, baby, after twenty-five years in this business, if all you've got to show for it is *Mogambo* and *The Hucksters* you might as well give up." When Reed jots something in his notebook, she retorts: "Don't tell me you're one of those people who always go around scribbling everything on little pieces of paper. Get rid of that. Don't take notes. Don't ask questions either because I probably won't answer any of them anyway. Just let Mama do all the talking." And she does, alas, to her own ruination. A gentleman, a standing for which not many writers qualify, would never have permitted so beautiful a woman, or even a very homely one, to expose herself to such sad disadvantage and then recount it for the public.

Tom Wolfe, who with Gay Talese is (or perhaps was, since he has long since turned to the novel as his genre of choice) one of the chief progenitors and exponents of the New Journalism, wrote what is perhaps its most famous single composition, "Radical Chic," about the composer and conductor Leonard Bernstein and his wife Felicia's party at their thirteen-room Park Avenue penthouse to raise money for twenty-one Black Panthers in prison for allegedly planning to blow up five New York department stores, New Haven Railroad facilities, and the Bronx botanical garden in the late 1960s. The result is as close as journalism is permitted to come to genius, dazzling in its detail, devastating in its effect. For some people, "Radical Chic" put an end to the rich unselfconsciously displaying their empty virtue by siding with the very people who, should their dreams come true, would be only too pleased to lead them to the guillotine.

That evening at the Bernsteins' apartment was an occasion on which some of the richest and most celebrated New Yorkers demonstrated how far from reality wealth and celebrity could place one. A journalist in the middle of the apartment—fellow name of Tom Wolfe—diligently taking notes on their foolishness, would eventually let everyone not there in on just how silly they were. He named names, some quite glittering names: Otto Preminger, Jean vanden Heuvel, Peter and Cheray Duchin, Barbara Walters, Bob Silvers, Mrs. Richard Avedon, Mrs. Arthur Penn, Richard Feigen, Frank and Donna Stanton, Elinor Guggenheimer, Julie Belafonte, Gail Lumet, Sheldon Harnick, and many others. At the end of Wolfe's account one is glad—delighted is more like it—not to have been among them.

Social hypocrisy has always been one of Tom Wolfe's great subjects, and it was never more perfectly placed in his kitchen, as the baseball sluggers say, than when he found himself in the Bernsteins' living room that evening. His fine eye for the nuttiness of social status was given an exhilarating workout. Here's Wolfe on the problem of finding the right servants for a party to raise money for a radical black organization:

> But it's all right. They're *white* servants, not Claude and Maude, but white South Americans. Lenny and Felicia are geniuses . . . Obviously, if you are giving a party for the Black Panthers, as Lenny and Felicia are this evening, and Richard Baron, the publisher, did before that; or for the Chicago Eight, such as the party Jean vanden Heuvel gave; or for the grape workers or Bernadette Devlin, such as the parties Andrew Stein gave; or the party for the Young Lords, such as the party Ellie Guggenheimer is giving next week in *her* Park Avenue duplex; or for the Indians or the SDS or the G.I. coffee shops or even for the Friends of the Earth—well, then, obviously you can't have a

Negro butler and maid, Claude and Maude, in uniform, circulating through the living room, the library, and the main hall serving drinks and canapés . . . Anyway, [the Bernsteins] have a house staff of three white South American servants . . . Can one comprehend how perfect that is, given . . . the times? Well, many of their friends can, and they ring up the Bernsteins and ask them to get South American servants for them, and the Bernsteins are so generous about it, so obliging, that people refer to them, good-naturedly and gratefully, as "the Spic and Span Employment Agency," with an easygoing humor, of course.

In an earlier day, a writer, coming upon a plum of such high human foolishness of the kind Tom Wolfe encountered at the Bernsteins' penthouse, might have turned the same material into fiction, providing a key for the knowing to unlock and thereby discover the true personages at the event. But in fiction it would be nowhere near so successful, so perfect, so, to choose an adjective that often appears before "gossip," juicy.

The element of self-abasement on Leonard Bernstein's part is nicely captured by Wolfe when he overhears the conductor say to one of the Panthers: "'When you walk into this house, into this building'" — and he gestures vaguely as if to take it all in, the moldings, the sconces, the Roquefort morsels rolled in crushed nuts, the servants, the elevator attendant and the doorman downstairs in their white dickeys, the marble lobby, the brass struts on the marquee out front — "'when you walk into this house, you must feel infuriated!'"

Bernstein's reputation — not as a composer but as a serious person — never survived Wolfe's account of that evening. His music is still played on classical music stations, where anniversaries of his birth and death are duly noted. His place in the line of twentieth-century composers and conductors remains reasonably high and has not been altered. But the journalistic account of his and his wife's behavior that night set him for eternity into that saddest of all social categories, a damn fool, too rich and famous to have the vaguest sense of how the world really works. "Radical Chic" is great journalism, but also gossip to the highest power. In fact, the two, in the hands of the New Journalists, seemed one and the same thing.

Tom Wolfe could of course have been crueler, for he left out altogether Leonard Bernstein's homosexuality, a well-known but not then generally proclaimed fact, for the date of "Radical Chic" was well before the age of outing, though I suspect Wolfe is too much the gent to have gone in for gay-bashing, especially when so much richer material was at hand.

In the loose form of literature known as the memoir, many people have taken to outing themselves, and not just on the subject of sexual preference. The memoir, as a form of self-gossip, taking time out to gossip about others, has become one of the common forms of recent years. In a notably egregious example, a former female associate of Bernard Madoff's not only admits to a love affair with the Ponzi specialist but informs us that his sexual apparatus was less than impressive. *Charmant!* A failed novelist describes his nervous breakdown. A woman writes about being sexually abused by her father. Another woman discourses at book length about her lifelong bout with depression, sparing no details. There's a lot of it going around, and it doesn't figure to end soon, the confession in which one often ends up confessing other people's sins, which comes to little more than gossip in a self-serving form. The phenomenon is reminiscent of a story I heard long ago of a man getting up in church in a small Arkansas town, the spirit upon him, confessing to having an affair with another woman, also in the congregation and sitting only a few pews away. He was saved for the Lord, but she, poor woman, had to leave town.

Diary

The first bit of public gossip—gossip, that is, about someone I did not know personally—that I can recall hearing arrived sometime in my early adolescence. Was I fourteen, fifteen, sixteen? I am not sure. Nor do I remember who told it to me. I do remember the words: "Randolph Scott is queerer than a three-dollar bill. Everybody knows that." This was the first such gossip about someone being secretly homosexual that I had ever heard. In those good/bad old days homosexual males were accommodatingly effeminate, on the model of Truman Capote, if not more flamboyant still. You didn't need a scorecard to tell the players. On the Capote standard, a more unlikely subject for such gossip than Randolph Scott could scarcely be imagined. Bronco-busting, fist-smashing, lean, leathery-faced, six feet two, Scott was the ideal type of the cowboy in American westerns, in which he was cast as the hero in more than a dozen.

Randolph Scott, homosexual—this was not an easy piece of gossip to digest. Yet everyone seemed to be in on it; it was apparently commonplace knowledge, like feeding a cold and starving a fever (or is it the other way around?), an urban legend that everyone was ready to believe but about which no one had persuasive proof, or at least any that I have ever heard.

In this instance the gossip about Randolph Scott's being gay acquired legs, as the journalists say, when he and Cary Grant moved in together in a house they called Bachelor Hall. Both men were said to be famously cheap, which is one possible reason they decided to share digs. Scott had been married (Grant married five times), and his adopted son Christopher wrote a book about him in which he devoted much space to denying the rampant gossip about his father's homosexuality. As for Cary Grant, he said that he "had nothing against gays, I'm just not one myself." Budd Boetticher, who directed Randolph Scott in six films, called the gossip about him, not to put too fine a point on it, "bullshit."

And there it remains: Randolph Scott, gay for eternity. Who knows the truth of the matter? "Ye shall know the truth," according to John 8:32, "and the truth shall make you free." Perhaps so, but sometimes it takes an awful long while.

14

Gay Gossip

> . . . the predatory and innuendo-filled air of the
> homosexual hothouse.
>
> — ROGER SCRUTON

WHILE NOT ALL homosexuals specialize in hot gossip, or even necessarily go in for it in a modest way, there is nonetheless a strain in gay culture that is rife with gossip, and for reasons that aren't difficult to understand. Until recent years, so many homosexuals — gay men especially — had had to hide the true nature of their sexuality and in doing so naturally developed a strong taste for spying out the hidden element in life; for those gay men whose homosexuality had not been revealed, few things could have been more significant than what was hidden. Leo Lerman, long the editorial director for Condé Nast magazines, who kept a gossip-laden journal for many years, wrote, in explanation of his doing so, that it was "because I am always interested in the disparity between the surface and what goes on underneath." This is, of course, the justification for most gossip: to tell what goes on underneath.

For the most part, the best gay gossip is, evidence suggests, conducted intramurally, guy to guy, or gay to gay. But then, this is true among all ethnic or in-groups. Thus the Jewish Isaiah Berlin to his mother about a fellow passenger on a transatlantic ship:

"He belongs to the vigorous pushing Jewish type which achieves a lot, and was illuminating both about Russia and about his own very gentlemanly people there." Thus in his play *Purlie Victorious,* the black playwright Ossie Davis has one of his black characters refer to another as "a disgrace to the Negro profession." One of the small but genuine benefits of belonging to a minority group is that one can put down and gossip about one's fellow group members with a clear conscience, an act not permitted to nonmembers of the group.

So gay men can mock one another, and also non-homosexual men and women, among themselves, often in a gay (in the old sense) and amusing spirit. Gay gossip can also seem more daring, more unashamed, in its wild playfulness. A gay character in Francis Wyndham's novella *The Other Garden* offers the following speculation:

> "Bet you dollars to doughnuts he's [said of another character in the novel] really queer as a coot (you can't fool Mother, dear!), but when I said so to Kay she got rather heated and swore it wasn't true. My guess is he's the pseudo-hearty kind who pretend to be normal and talk about the place being terribly, terribly manly. *Mee-ow!* I sound just like Ros Russell in *The Women.* I can't think why I said that about Sandy—it just popped out! I've always sworn I would never turn into one of those dreary old queens who try to make out that everybody else is queer too—no, dear, that sort of behaviour is definitely not my *tasse de thé*—so I take it all back."

Later in the novella the same character reports:

> "I've got lots of fascinating scandal to tell you . . . I picked up a Yank the other day who worked in a big actors' agency in Hollywood before he was drafted, and he told me all the dirt about the sex life of the stars. I bet you'll never guess what Joan Crawford's favorite kind is. *Well,* my dear . . . this person says that what she really likes best is to pee on people! An actor friend of his had an affair with her and was simply terrified when she suddenly stood up on the bed and loomed above him with her

legs apart. When it dawned on him what she was going to do, he said, 'Wait just one moment, please,' and dashed off to the bathroom to fetch one of those waterproof shower-caps!"

In his day, Truman Capote was one of the finest purveyors of gay gossip. "Truman," wrote Leo Lerman in his journal, "told me so many dreadful things about everybody. It's wonderful how Truman acquires bits of information and then passes them off as his own." Capote's letters are a cornucopia of candor aimed at amusing. "Jackie [Kennedy] et moi spent the whole night talking about sex" is a nice specimen. Capote, in a gossipy letter, claims a dalliance with Montgomery Clift. His most gossip-rich letters are written to gay friends. "I've liked it here [in Portofino]," he writes to a friend named Andrew Lyndon, "and have done a lot of work, but in August [of 1953] everything became too social—and I *do* mean social—the Windsors (morons), the Luces (morons plus), Garbo (looking like death with a suntan), the Oliviers (they let her [Vivien Leigh] out [of an insane asylum]), Daisy Fellowes [heiress to the Singer Sewing Machine fortune] . . .—then Cecil [Beaton] and John Gielgud came to stay with us, and we went to Venice on Arthur Lopez's yacht—whence I've just come back. Oh, yes, I forgot Noël Coward." In his diary for the same date, Noël Coward notes, "We have gossiped with Truman Capote," and one can only imagine how wild that conversation might have been.

Gossip among what Truman Capote called "the whole Lavender Hill mob" tends to be at its most wicked when a strong whiff of hatred is admixed. Gore Vidal, a man much of whose writing is stoked by hatred, always went out of his way to say vicious gossipy things about Capote, so much so that once, during the filming of *Murder by Death,* in which Capote had an acting part, when a six-hundred-pound chandelier came loose from the ceiling and smashed a table on the set, Capote remarked, "Gore's got to be somewhere in the wings."

Vidal lashes Capote unrelentingly through gossip, sometimes inserted into his book reviewing, more often through the many interviews he has given over the years. (The envenomed gossipy interview, usually on a television talk show, is a Gore Vidal specialty.) Writing about Tennessee Williams, Vidal takes time out to recall that Capote used to entertain the playwright and him with "mischievous fantasies about the great. Apparently the very sight of him was enough to cause lifelong heterosexual men to tumble out of unsuspected closets. When Capote refused to surrender his virtue to a drunk Errol Flynn, '*Errol threw all my suitcases out of the window of the Beverly Wilshire Hotel!*'" Vidal caps the story by adding, "I should note here that the young Capote was no less attractive in his person then than he is today," when, of course, he was distinctly unbeautiful. Vidal also reports Tennessee Williams once noting that Capote could be a fine companion, and had not yet "turned bitchy."

On a bitchy note of his own, Vidal, in 1974 to an interviewer from the magazine *Fag Rag*, complains that the only kind of homosexual writer the American reading public is willing "to put up with is a freak like Capote, who has the mind of a Kansas housewife, likes gossip, and gets all shuddery when she thinks about boys murdering people" (this last a reference to Capote's *In Cold Blood*, a better and more widely read book than any Vidal ever wrote). When asked by another interviewer about Capote's wealth, Vidal replies that Capote has no real money but lives as if he had: "He thinks he's Bunny Mellon . . . He thinks he's a very rich Society Lady, and spends a great deal of money." As for Capote's gifts, "a gift for publicity is the most glittering star in his diadem." He's "our literature's Suzy [Knickerbocker]" and "wears with a certain panache the boa of the late Louella Parsons." (Any of this said by a heterosexual would have resulted in mass protests.) Capote is also "ruthlessly unoriginal," Vidal writes, and "plundered Carson McCullers for *Other Voices, Other Rooms,* abducted Isherwood's Sally Bowles for *Breakfast at Tiffany's,*" and then turned to journalism, "the natural realm of those without creative imagination."

One of Capote's own specialties was gossiping in public; the more public the place, the more it seemed to stimulate him. On *The Tonight Show,* he told Johnny Carson and an audience of millions that he thought the best-selling novelist Jacqueline Susann looked like nothing so much as "a truck driver in drag." At the time when Sammy Davis Jr. was riding high as an entertainer, Capote, from the comfort of Carson's couch, announced that "I find him excruciatingly boring" and went on to say that he couldn't possibly understand what anyone could see in so overly energetic but otherwise unoriginal a man.

When Capote published a chapter of a novel long in progress called *Unanswered Prayers* in *Esquire,* a chapter mocking and reporting gossip about the thinly disguised wealthy women — Babe Paley, Nan Kemperer, Slim Keith, and others — into whose company he had worked so hard to insinuate himself, these same women cut him off, leaving him puzzled and crushed. Why they would do so seemed to have baffled Capote, who never completed his novel and whose brain had by then probably been stewed to mush by alcohol and pills.

Leo Lerman's, like much old-line gay gossip, specializes in the lowdown on divas, operatic and otherwise, and who is secretly gay, or possibly bisexual. He informs us that Yul Brynner was bisexual, having had a fling with Hurd Hatfield, the star of the movie *The Picture of Dorian Gray.* From the horse's (that would be Truman Capote's) mouth, so, according to Lerman, was Steve McQueen bisexual. Arturo Toscanini did not approve of his daughter's marriage to Vladimir Horowitz, who, in any case, "didn't love her, since he wanted men." While "talking to his children, Lenny [Bernstein] pinched my ass a lot."

In the heterosexual world, Lerman reports that Aristotle Onassis slept with Lee Radziwill, before "Jackie grabbed him." Mary McCarthy, he recounts, made an unsuccessful attempt to seduce Lionel Trilling, in the hope of rising to the top of the world of New York intellectuals. Diana Trilling believed her son hated her. Lerman tells about the heavy drinking of Dixie Lee Crosby, the wife of Bing, who one day while drunk "kicked one of her little boys in the stomach so hard that he had to have an operation."

A more charming class of gay gossip comes from Noël Coward, whose information didn't seem soaked in the poisonous waters of personal animosity. In his diary—and diaries, by their nature, are a form of gossip, for as the English diarist Chips Channon wrote, "What is more dull than a discreet diary?"—Coward speaks of Vivien Leigh's carrying on after Laurence Olivier leaves her for the actress Joan Plowright: "Vivien has appeared in London and is busily employed in making a cracking ass of herself. She is right round the bend again, as I suspected, and looks ghastly. I suspect there is far less mental instability about it than most people seem to think . . . She is almost inarticulate with drink and spitting vitriol about everyone and everything."

Coward is especially good on actresses: "Marlene [Dietrich] made an entrance looking ravishing and was quite entrancing for an hour. Then she became boring and over-egocentric . . . I suddenly feel a wave of relief that I hadn't agreed to do an Australian tour with her. I am quite sure she would have driven me barmy." He travels to Chicago to see Tallulah Bankhead in his play *Private Lives* and reports in a letter to a friend that "I understand Tallulah does everything but stuff a kipper up her twot but is playing to smash capacity!" The next evening, he reports seeing her in the play in the company of Alfred Lunt and Lynn Fontanne, and when Fontanne congratulates her in her dressing room, Tallulah replies: "'I don't give a fuck about you and Alfred. It's only Noël I am worrying about.' She said it in no way maliciously but merely as a statement of fact! Fortunately it was all such a gel of effusiveness and fun that nobody minded but I thought you would like to know it as an example of Dix-Huitième courtesy and tact." There, I would say, one has the best of gay gossip, exhibiting, in one sweep, outrageousness, comedy, and charm.

What can make gay gossip so wild and amusing is that homosexual men, having long thought themselves outside the realm of middle-class respectability, have achieved a nice distancing, a spectatorial view of so-called normal life, which is at heart comic. This same distancing, viewing everything through different binoculars, often results in lending gossip a witty twist. It gives the best gay gossip its mordancy, suggesting as it often does that life really is a sham, don't you know, and how amusing it is to pierce it by observing people playing out their hopeless little pageants of pretense and hypocrisy. Oscar Wilde's entire oeuvre seems to be about little else.

Tennessee Williams, whose plays are so heavy in their symbolic earnestness, had the light gay gossip touch to a fine degree. "He loved sexual gossip, especially about other writers," reported his friend Dotson Rader. Williams repeats a story about William Faulkner's being broken up because Jean Stein, the daughter of Jules Stein, who controlled Universal Pictures, wouldn't marry him. "Of course," he concludes, putting aside Faulkner's belief that Jean Stein rejected him because he wasn't Jewish, that the real story was "Jean didn't want to marry him because he was a hell of a lot older than her, was a drunk, and she didn't look forward to spending her married life in Oxford, Mississippi, where the only thing to do is watch the cows go by."

Williams recounts the story of Clifton Webb's grief over the death of his mother, and his claim that the reason he, Webb, remained a bachelor until well into his seventies was because his marrying would have hurt her. *"Shock's* more like it," Williams says. "Clifton Webb didn't marry because he was as gay as the Seventh Fleet, and everybody knew it, including him." Webb apparently made a great thing about his sorrow at his mother's death, until Noël Coward "shook Cliffy and said, 'Darling, pull yourself together! It is not unreasonable to be orphaned at seventy.'"

The Clifton Webb story elides nicely into a story about one Jimmy Donohue, who "was a very rich, very nice queen who was a Woolworth heiress and had had a short-lived affair with Cliffy many years ago. And then for a few years he was the boyfriend of the Duchess of Windsor, although it was strictly nonphysical." Such gay gossip holds out the promise of pulling back the curtain on an intimate scene, which one may or may not believe but is nonetheless amusing to contemplate. The entire operation assumes that people are everywhere leading secret lives, that appearance and reality are wildly incongruent.

Gay gossip took a tragic turn when AIDS cut its black swath through gay life, and gossip often centered on who had AIDS and who was hiding it. The great dancer Rudolf Nureyev, for example, denied he had AIDS, and then died of it. In an instance of gossip through fiction, in Saul Bellow's novel *Ravelstein,* the eponymous hero, a figure not merely based on but to everyone's knowledge precisely the philosopher and University of Chicago teacher Allan Bloom, is homosexual and described as dying of AIDS. When the book was published, many of Bloom's friends and former students were outraged that Bellow would portray Bloom in this way, arguing that he died instead from the effects of Guillain-Barré Syndrome, an auto-immune disease affecting the nervous system, from which he had earlier suffered. No one ever said it aloud, but it was important to Bloom's friends, none of whom denied his homosexuality, that he died of an auto-immune disease rather than one associated with sexual promiscuity. They preferred Bloom to have been an important intellectual figure who also happened to be gay, rather than a gay man who also happened to be an important intellectual figure. Did Bellow know for sure that Bloom died of AIDS, or was he engaging in that form of speculation also known as gossip? The question of the cause of Allan Bloom's death has yet to be cleared up with any certainty, and it dallies in the limbo of gossip.

In a culture in which people rather enjoy gossiping about themselves, gossip itself changes radically. In gay gossip, these changes are on emphatic display in the writing of Edmund White, a gay writer a generation younger than Williams, Capote, Lerman, and Coward. Previously people who were gay tended to keep their homosexuality off to the side—they didn't feature it, even when they had no difficulty owning up to it—but we now have people who, like the character in the play *Purlie Victorious,* might almost be said to be in the homosexual profession, and Edmund White is one of them. White writes about his own homosexuality freely and prolifically; without it he would be deprived of a subject, wouldn't really quite exist as a writer.

All but agreeing with this, White, in a recent memoir called *City Boy* (2009), writes that if he had been straight, "I would never have turned toward writing with a burning desire to confess, to understand, to justify myself in the eyes of others." White gossips as much about himself as he does about others. In this memoir the young Edmund White, freshly out of the closet, recounts his move to New York in the 1960s and a life of nearly full-time promiscuity. "Brandy Alexander, a famous drag queen, said to me at a party, 'Ed White, everyone wants you, you're the universal ball.'" He describes some of the wilder gay bars and discos and leather scenes, remarking almost by the way that "sado-masochism [in the late 1960s] still sounded perverted and ever so slightly tacky—sort of New Jersey." He offers brief accounts of the generation of gay and lesbian writers and artists just ahead of his own (White was born in 1940). Among those he mentions are Elizabeth Bishop, Jan Morris, Robert Mapplethorpe, John Ashbery, Susan Sontag, James Merrill, and Harold Brodkey.

White's own sexual propensities are filled in. He informs us that he is "a bottom" and had "always been an apostle of promiscuity." Prose snapshots of his homosexual bouts are provided: "I went to bed with John [Hohnsbeen, previously the lover of the architect Philip Johnson] once, but I'm afraid that I wasn't aggressive enough to interest him." Bruce Chatwin, a writer who attracted much literary attention until his death from AIDS in 1989, "with his bright, hard eyes and his odorless WASP body and flickering, ironic smile and his general derring-do instantly groped me while we were still standing just inside the door, and a minute later we'd shed our clothes and were still standing. We had sex in the most efficient way, we put our clothes back on, and we never repeated the experience with each other." White mentions, in passing, having gone to bed with a drunk John Ashbery and his boyfriend.

But in the end candor does not in itself create interest and is devoid of allure. A man gossiping about himself is always insufficiently amusing. This is because self-gossip violates the equation that holds that gossip is two or more people telling things about a third that the latter would prefer not be known. Edmund White is one person telling about himself, and he wants everyone to know about it. Charm departs and, as the old song has it, the thrill is gone.

Diary

Mortimer Adler, the founder with Robert Hutchins of the publishing project called Great Books of the Western World, held firmly to the belief that everyone was, in his word, "educable." And not educable merely, but able to read and benefit from the richly complex Great Books. This, for him, was a matter of faith, an article of belief. His entire career was founded upon it.

I worked for a few years for Adler when he took over the intellectual redesign of the *Encyclopaedia Britannica*. He was an intellectual bully and a man with an impressively blind eye to the environment in which he operated. But one of the side benefits of working for this very energetic, too deeply concentrated man of high but rough-hewn intellect was having a coign of vantage on his irrationality. This irrationality was especially amusing in light of Adler's powerful insistence on the crucial element of reason and logic in life.

Plentiful were the anecdotes of Adler's comic irrationality. There was the story of his wife's asking him to hang a picture in their Chicago Gold Coast apartment, and Adler, owning no hammer, walking out to swank Michigan Avenue to buy one. No hardware store being available, he stepped into Dunhill, a favorite haunt, and bought instead a gold-plated showerhead, which he brought home to hammer in the nail needed to hang the picture.

There was the story of Adler's pursuing a young woman and setting out to write a love poem to her. His secretary noticed him composing on a yellow legal pad, scribbling madly away, crumpling up sheet after sheet of failed efforts. Finally the poet manqué declared he was off for lunch at the Tavern

Club. His secretary, her curiosity piqued by what he may have been writing, looked down at the pad on Adler's desk, upon which she discovered a single word, the beginning of his love poem: "Whereas."

But the best story, one long kept under wraps, was told to me by a man who was Adler's assistant when he had his office in San Francisco. Unhappy in his first marriage, Adler one day called his wife from a hotel room to inform her that he wanted a divorce. (Phoning in your divorce is a nice touch.) Not long thereafter he was seen in the company of a woman much younger and quite a bit gaudier than he. The philosopher of the Great Books, one of the leading exponents of the doctrines of Saint Thomas Aquinas, a man of doubtless towering IQ, was clearly smitten. He soon announced his intention to marry this woman.

Adler's friends were suspicious, and hired detectives to follow the young woman and the man she called her brother. Adler meanwhile took out a large insurance policy naming her as sole beneficiary. You will have anticipated me here when I report that the young woman's brother was her boyfriend, and the two were plotting to kill the philosopher. The police were called in, Adler was informed of the plot, the woman and her boyfriend were dealt with, and everything was hushed up lest scandal result. The moral of the story? Might it be that, after all, perhaps not everyone is entirely educable?

GREAT GOSSIPS OF THE
WESTERN WORLD, III

The Yenta

She thinks of herself as a journalist, and, true enough, she has worked for the news divisions of the major television networks. She has interviewed twelve — perhaps by now it is thirteen — American presidents and countless leaders of foreign countries. For a time she worked as a television news anchor — a job held by Edward R. Murrow, Walter Cronkite, and John Chancellor, respected figures who gave the impression of high seriousness — and was the first woman to do so. Her connections, her credentials, her bona fides, her impressively high ratings, all are there, perfectly in order. Why then, in spite of all this, and after a long and successful career, money and accolades flowing in, does she nonetheless seem like nothing so much as a yenta, a female blabbermouth and busybody.

She, of course, is Barbara Walters.

Barbara Walters was the daughter of Lou Walters, a nightclub impresario famous in his day, the 1930s through the 1940s, for founding and running the nightclubs in Manhattan and Miami called the Latin Quarter. A high roller, Lou Walters, and like most such men, his fortunes, roller-coaster-like, went up and down. The ride was not always easy on his womenfolk: Barbara's mother, her three-years-older retarded sister Jackie, and Barbara herself. Guilt and insecurity are the leitmotifs of the memoir Barbara published called *Audition,* a title meant to suggest that she is perpetually in the tenuous condition of trying out for a part, no matter how fully arrived she may seem to everyone else. Barbara, as she herself recounts, was always worried about not doing enough for her family, especially her sister, and was no less worried about being knocked down from the greasy pole of her profession up which she has so persistently and aggressively climbed.

Troubled, to put it gently, was Barbara's childhood: many moves from apartment to apartment owing to her father's rocky business, not seeing enough of her father who worked late hours, feeling the frightening reverberations from the tensions of her parents' shaky marriage, having to drag along her sister, of whom she was half ashamed and fully guilty for the shame she felt. Fearful of rejection, Barbara didn't run with the first circle of girls in school, but chose the second circle. Later, when she wanted to go to Wellesley, she was put on the waiting list. She wound up at Sarah Lawrence, another second-circle choice.

Sarah Lawrence College, in the late 1940s and early '50s, turned out to be just the right school for Barbara. Progressive in its aims, it was more than progressive, it was wonderfully avant-cuckoo in its methods. In those days Barbara wanted to be an actress, so she majored in theater. Her classes, as she describes them, sound very soft, spongy really. The one science course she took was The Psychology of Art, for which she wrote a term paper on love. The classes were small: six to no more than a dozen students. "What we did," she reports of Sarah Lawrence, "was talk. And discuss. And talk some more. I learned to ask questions and to listen." Sounds, the whole four years, rather like an extended Barbara Walters special. "I learned never to be afraid of speaking up. Every student's point of view was taken seriously, and no one ever said, 'That's stupid' or 'That's irrelevant.'" Perhaps someone should have done; Walters's career might have turned out very differently.

Of Sarah Lawrence she notes that "none of us [she and her fellow students at the then all-female college] needed a psychiatrist because we lived in group therapy every day. There were no secrets among us, no privacy." Which only shows again how perfect the college was for Barbara, for her work would always have something of the warm glow of the therapeutic, of the bull session with the girls, of the therapist's couch. Her entire career, like an extension of Sarah Lawrence days, was devoted to eliminating secrets and thereby privacy.

Barbara had had some success acting in college plays, but when she auditioned for parts in New York, some of them set up for her through her father's Broadway connections, she found herself overwhelmed by fear of rejection. Instead she took various jobs in public relations. One of them was writing publicity for the local affiliate of NBC-TV, which gave her entrée into television. The spread of television, which put an end to her father's career as an impresario—with the rise of television, people went out at night a great deal less, which killed the nightclub business—was of course the beginning of her own much grander one.

Like so many young women of her generation, Barbara married in her twenties—a less than passionate marriage, in her account of it—a man named Bob Katz, with whom she discovered she hadn't much to talk about. (Not a good candidate for a Barbara Walters special, Mr. Katz.) This was to be the first of her three marriages. She also tells us that she had three miscarriages, and so, during her second marriage, to a man named Lee Gruber, she adopted a child.

Between marriages, Barbara was seen around New York with Roy Cohn, one of the most despised men in the country owing to his work as Senator Joseph McCarthy's axman in his Communist-hunting campaign. She and Cohn were never romantically entangled; he was, as was later revealed, a homosexual (Cohn died of AIDS in 1986). She says that he used her as a beard to cover his homosexuality, which she wasn't aware of at the time. He proposed marriage to her more than once; at one point, when he had bought a townhouse on the East Side of New York, in which he promised to install her sister and her now down-on-their-luck parents, she claims she was tempted. And oh yes, Roy Cohn, Barbara, ever the good gossip, also tells us, had a number of face-lifts.

Throughout her memoir Barbara provides lots of such gossipy tidbits. She reports that the actress Maureen O'Sullivan was "on a steady diet of prescription pills," which made her brief time on the *Today* show less than successful. A figure around Washington named Joan Braden used the lure of sex to secure interviews and scoops as a journalist; she was, Barbara tells us, Robert McNamara's "so-called travelling companion, after his wife's death," and supposedly "had a fling with Robert Kennedy." A colleague named Pat Fontaine had a drinking problem. The actor George Sanders's meanness wasn't just in the roles he played; he was a genuine lout. She drags in the old chestnut about John F. Kennedy bonking Angie Dickinson, informs us of Grace Kelly's unhappiness as a princess in Monaco, gives us the lowdown on John Wayne's diddling his young female assistant, and oh so much more. But then, gossiping about herself, she also tells us that she had a lengthy love affair with Senator Edward Brooke. A journalist's work, it sometimes seems, is never done.

Barbara Walters achieved celebrity by interviewing celebrity. She was famous enough to have her slight speech impediment mocked on *Saturday Night Live* by Gilda Radner as a character called Baba Wawa. Celebrity, carefully orchestrated, can take a person a long way, and Barbara has been a Toscanini of her own renown. She became the first female news anchor, sharing the job with Harry Reasoner, though her salary, to his great chagrin, was larger than his.

Such was Barbara's fame that heads of state, the biggest movie stars, people caught up in serious crimes, wished to be interviewed by her. They wanted their say before her enormous audience. She refers to landing an interview with an immensely famous person as a "get," but she was herself becoming a big get on her own. When in power, Richard Nixon helped set up interviews for her. He had his motives, she hers. "We used each other," she writes, "and that's the way it has worked out with so many guests I've talked to over the years. People come on TV because they want the exposure and a forum to advance whatever it is they want to advance. And I want something, too—the interview." One dirty hand washes the other.

In television, high ratings are of an importance equal to oxy-
gen for human life: without either, death quickly follows. High
ratings were never Barbara's problem; she understood how to get
them. In 1974, *Newsweek* put her on its cover, claiming that her
interview questions are "dumdum bullets swaddled in angora."
Dumb-dumb might have been a little more like it. No one listens
to Barbara Walters to learn about the delicate balance of power
in Europe, the fate of the economy, or the rise of Islamofascism.
They watch her in the hope that she will ask the not necessarily
outrageous but the pointedly vulgar question. And she does not
let her viewers down. She asks Fidel Castro if he is secretly married, and Prince Philip if his wife, Queen Elizabeth II, would soon
be likely to leave the throne so that her son could become King.
She queries Barbara Bush on her depression, asks Boris Yeltsin if
he drinks too much, Vladimir Putin if he has ever killed anyone,
Muammar Qaddafi if he is insane, and dings Martha Stewart with
"Why do so many people hate you?" She asks Hillary Clinton,
after her husband's divertissements with an intern is revealed,
"How could you stay in this marriage?" Then she turns the dial
a notch further and asks, "What if he does it again?" She reports
that "I knew it would be hard for her to answer, but I had to ask."

"I had to ask" is a not uncommon formulation of Barbara's.
To her dismay, she never interviewed a pope. If a pope agreed to
an interview with Barbara, before it was over she would doubtless get around to asking, "Holy Father, have you no regrets about
never having had children?" Camilla Parker Bowles, the Prince
of Wales's second wife, refused to do an interview with Barbara,
who no doubt would have asked what it's like to have a prince tell
you that he wishes he were a tampon inside you. She would, you
understand, have had to ask.

Barbara Walters must know that this vulgar streak, asking the
low questions that are on the mass mind, is her bread and caviar.
She also knows not to step out of her intellectual league. An interview with Elizabeth Taylor is going to top one with any world
leader you might care to mention. How does Barbara know?
Simple enough: the ratings tell her so. All very well to interview

Henry Kissinger (a friend, it turns out, but then very few famous people aren't her friend), but Maria Callas on being deserted by Aristotle Onassis for Jackie (soon to be O) Kennedy rings the ratings gong more resoundingly. Late in her memoir she complains rather sniffily that "since the Britney Spearses of the world and sensational crime stories became the big ratings draws, international political leaders . . . have come to be considered dull fare." But of course she knew this long before; perhaps as much as anyone in America, she may be said to have contributed to its coming about.

She comes across as a sensitive, caring woman in her television appearances—the nation's therapist, our Barbara—but she also has a taste for vengeance. Two anchors who never cottoned to her, Frank McGee at NBC and Harry Reasoner at ABC, thinking her insufficiently intelligent and thus lowering the tone of their profession, get her stiletto through belated—posthumous, actually—gossip. She reports that McGee, thought to be a happily married man, toward the end of his life "plunged into a flagrant love affair with a young black production assistant named Mamye, and had left his wife to live with her," adding that Mamye was not "particularly pretty." Reasoner is hung out to dry for his pettiness and backbiting. In her memoir, Barbara front-bites him.

Barbara Walters has all these years been living out a secret drama. In it she is a feminist pioneer who broke down all the masculine barriers and, at great personal cost, cleared the way for Diane Sawyer, Katie Couric, and all the other female anchors. In a line of work specializing in high pretension, why should only men be allowed to score big money as empty trench coats?

Barbara claims no one knows her politics, that when she is interviewing famous murderers, thugs, or thieves she holds back judgment—at least she does so during the interview. She will, though, let us know that she feels deeply, very deeply. Of the parents of Ronald Goldman, the young man killed with O. J. Simpson's wife, she tells us that she "ached for them." She goes in for what in the business isn't but ought to be called "the weepies"; interviewing the families of the victims of 9/11, she lets us know how wrenching it was for *her*. Repeatedly she reports that she has stayed in touch with men and women she has interviewed, to make sure we all know that she doesn't merely use these people as another "get," useful to score yet another ratings hit. She's very human, she wants us to know, and not in the least corrupted by the somewhat scurrilous job that has provided her such a smooth ride through life.

Some things even Barbara will not do. The thought of her interviewing O. J. Simpson and helping him make money on a book sickens her. She finds Paris Hilton's family's request for money for an interview with their daughter "shoddy." Complicated negotiations were conducted over money for Barbara to interview the former White House intern Monica Lewinsky. "Of course I wanted to do the interview," she reports, "but I was not so ambitious that I didn't have a conscience." As part of her enticement pitch, she tells Monica Lewinsky, "I can give you the forum and the opportunity to present yourself with the greatest dignity." Monica goes for it, and the interview turns out to be "the most watched special in the history of television" and "also the biggest 'get' of my career." Monica Lewinsky's dignity, never really up for redemption, was not a keynote of the interview.

In the spirit of the times, Barbara gossips about herself. Well, not really about herself but about members of her family. She talks about the complications of her parents' marriage, about the difficulties of her retarded sister, and finally, most lengthily, about her only daughter, Jackie. (The perfect daughter for Barbara, a mischievous mind might say, might have been Monica Lewinsky herself.) Raising Jackie is all sweetness and light, till one day the girl turns up missing lots of classes at the Dalton School, doing drugs, and hanging with the wrong sort of boys. At one point the kid runs to ground. But it is a story with a happy ending: Jackie is eventually found, detoxed, deprogrammed, and is now back in the game, running a "small residential outdoor therapy program" in Maine for wayward girls. Barbara "supported her in every possible way . . . and our relationship became closer and closer." Why keep the whole thing quiet? Why suppress an inspirational story? Why observe the thinnest desire for privacy? She pitched the story of her and her daughter's saga to NBC's *Dateline,* which bought it.

Barbara's last big shot has been a daytime program called *The View,* in which four or five women, neither notable for their reticence nor overly concerned about their dignity, talk about the "personal aspects of our lives." ABC, Barbara allows, would go with the idea for the show only if she agreed to appear regularly on it. On *The View,* celebrity guests, yearning to keep the flame of their fame alive, come on and are invited to do as the regular members do. "Just plop yourself down on our couch," Barbara writes, "and discuss your film and your sex life." What fun! And another ratings winner for Barbara.

Pretty amazing, all of it. Why has this woman, whose charm is not always evident, but who has lots of energy and boundless ambition yet no obvious talent to accompany either, why has Barbara Walters become, with the possible exception of Oprah Winfrey, the most famous woman in America? She has gone, as the Victorians used to say — though no one, surely, could be less Victorian than Barbara — from strength to strength. Now in her eighties, she admits to being a little tired of the game. "Celebrities with problems were becoming less appealing to me," she notes, and the competition for "gets" becoming tougher all the time, with Diane Sawyer and Katie Couric and Oprah now on the hunt.

Give Barbara her due: week after week, year after year, she has created gossip through the simple agency of asking the most tasteless questions of famous people, who were themselves tasteless enough to answer her. Not just anyone could have brought it off. Yet to her it all seems to have come so naturally.

Diary

My first book, *Divorced in America: Marriage in an Age of Possibility,* was published in 1974, the same year that *People* magazine began publication. Because mine was in good part a personal book—half of it taking up the issues, questions, and problems entailed in divorce, the other half chronicling my own experience going through a divorce—the editors of *People* must have thought that here was a subject made for their magazine. A young woman reporter was sent out to interview me, with an amusing Hungarian photographer driving a tan Mercedes in tow. They must have thought they had a good gossipy story, but what they hadn't counted on was that I lived, by their lights, an abnormally quiet life.

The reporter wondered if they might take pictures of my then lady friend, who would a few years later become my wife, walking along the beach of Lake Michigan. But publicity to my friend was of no interest; in fact, she thought it more than a touch vulgar, especially publicity of the clichéd thoughtful-couple-walking-along-the-beach variety.

As for me, I ostensibly had no life to speak of. I chiefly read and sat in front of a typewriter, tapping away at essays, stories, articles, and book reviews. For complicated reasons, I had custody of my children, but I didn't want them dragged into an issue of *People,* and I made that plain at the outset. I did in those days play tennis, so the Hungarian photographer took scores of shots of me whapping away at tennis balls. The reporter sensed that the real story must have been my ex-wife, who no longer lived in the same city I did, and she wondered if she might be allowed to get in touch with her. I had taken the greatest care to leave my ex-wife out of my book, never blaming her for any share in the breakup of the marriage or speaking of any flaws or weaknesses in her character; I wanted above all not to seem the typically disgruntled partner to a divorce. So despite relentless pursuit on the reporter's part, I refused to reveal the whereabouts of my ex-wife, thus depriving *People*'s story of any gossip value whatsoever. I was the subject and cause of an extremely boring story—perhaps, I like to think, the most boring ever to appear in its pages.

When the story ran, and I was half surprised that it did, it contained two photographs, one of me washing out socks in a bathroom sink, the other of me stretched out on my bed reading a biography of Chekhov. *People* has long since failed to pay me another visit.

III

PRIVATE BECOME PUBLIC

15

Caught in the Net

The Internet is democracy's revenge on democracy.

— MOLLY HASKELL

I RECENTLY READ AN excellent novel called *Crampton Hodnet* by Barbara Pym whose plot, action, and denouement are all triggered by gossip. Gossip is the theme of the book. The subject has to do with a middle-aged Oxford don, feeling himself much taken for granted by his wife and daughter, who begins what will be an unconsummated love affair with an attractive student. His having been seen in a teashop and elsewhere with the student is reported to the don's aunt, a great busybody of a dowager, who takes it upon herself to report this to his wife. The don's averring his love for the student in, of all places, the British Museum is overheard by an assistant librarian at the Bodleian, who tells it to his own mother, who also reports it to the don's wife. Barbara Pym, a novelist of comic subtlety and lovely detachment, captures how delighted everyone is to have these morsels of gossip and the pleasure it gives to serve them around with a heavy dollop of moral indignation. One also gets the sense that gossip traditionally has worked best in a small, one might even say tight, community, such as the north Oxford of her novel provides.

One of the characters, the assistant librarian at the Bodleian, keeps his mother and others "entertained with spiteful bits of gossip." The dowager aunt views passing on gossip as a duty of a kind, noting that "there are some things that one cannot let pass without comment. It is a duty one has to other people, not always a pleasant or an easy duty, but one which must be performed." The assistant librarian's mother claims that "we do not tell stories about people for our own amusement," which is partially true, for condemnation of other people ranks higher as a priority than mere amusement for the characters in this novel. The don in *Crampton Hodnet* being gossiped about does not win much sympathy as a victim, for, about to go off on a trip with a colleague he does not much like, he thinks that "at least they would be able to have a good talk about old times, rejoicing over those of their contemporaries who had not fulfilled their early promise and belittling those who had." The novelist's point here is that the man being gossiped about has himself a taste for gossip. Pym has another character "often notice that clever people were inclined to be fond of spiteful gossip." Too true, of course.

Smart and charming though Barbara Pym's novel is, one cannot help but feel something akin to nostalgia for the kind of old-fashioned gossip it chronicles. Nostalgia because, though such gossip doubtless still exists in small, isolated places, the older traditions of gossip have now been altered, and radically. What has changed everything is the Internet, one of whose clearest side effects has been greatly to speed the spread of gossip. Endless are the websites devoted to gossip. Gawker.com, TMZ.com, Pagesix.com are only among the most prominent for general celebrity gossip, and there are scores of others dedicated to realms of more specialized gossip.

On April 1, 2010, the *New York Times* published a lengthy article under the headline "The Walter Winchells of Cyberspace." The article featured nine people, all of them in their twenties or early thirties, who are attempting to earn a living by purveying gossip in finance, show business, real estate, teen life, fashion, the Ivy League, urban culture industries, sports, you name it, all exclusively over the Internet.

As every academic subject has its politics, so does every division and kind of work have its gossip, and lots of it now appears on the Internet. Early in the *Times* article, its author, Alex Williams, writes what is becoming truer and truer every day: "The line between 'reporter' and 'blogger,' 'gossip' and 'news,' has blurred almost beyond distinction." He goes on to note that blogging has become "a career path in its own right, offering visibility, influence, and an actual paycheck."

Even e-mail, by its very nature of being something dashed off, without the forethought of an old-fashioned letter, is gossip-prone; one writes something indiscreet about another person in an e-mail, says oh what the hell, clicks Send, and *whoosh,* off it goes. Then there are the social network websites: Facebook, Friendster, MySpace, MyLife, and others, all highly charged conveyors of gossip in the realm of personal life, sometimes accompanied by photographs of their authors, drunk or naked or in other forms of moral deshabille. Add to all this the blogs, hundreds of thousands of them, in fact by now millions of them. Blogs can be many things, but they function chiefly as engines of opinionation. And where there is unbridled opinion — uncensored and served up without established standards or responsible checks — gossip is likely to be not far behind.

No one is safe from gossip on the Internet. An example is Elena Kagan, the most recent U.S. Supreme Court justice. While Justice Kagan was under consideration for the Court, in his Daily Dish website the journalist Andrew Sullivan, who runs a much-visited blog and is also a gay activist, brought up the question of whether Kagan, who was then fifty and never married, might be a lesbian. He felt it important to know. "It is no more of an empirical question than whether she is Jewish," Sullivan wrote. "We know she is Jewish, and it is a fact simply and rightly put in the public square. If she were to hide her Jewishness, it would seem rightly odd, bizarre, anachronistic, even arguably self-critical or self-loathing. And yet we have been told by many that she is gay . . . and no one will ask directly if this is true and no one in the administration will tell us definitively."

Andrew Sullivan's "item" about Elena Kagan was immediately picked up by CBS, which put it on its website. All sorts of websites, from gay to wing nut, followed. Next television got into the act by mentioning the item. The *Washington Post* journalist Sally Quinn went on *The O'Reilly Factor* to report that in Washington conversation this was Topic Number One. Bill O'Reilly claimed that he hated this story, but, come to think of it, as he evidently did, it was important to know whether Kagan was a lesbian, for if she were to be confirmed as a justice, she would at some time in her tenure be asked to pass judgment on gay marriage.

The White House now pitched in, denying that Elena Kagan was gay. This set off a bevy of further online comments on the homophobia of the Obama administration. (What's wrong with her being gay?) Suddenly everything was out of control, and all one could think of in connection with Elena Kagan, who until then had apparently had a calm life and an exemplary career, was whether or not she was a lesbian. None of this would have happened if the Internet hadn't begun the greasy ball rolling.

If Elena Kagan is gay, surely she is well within her rights, if she so chooses, to keep it to herself. But the damage has been done. No longer will it be possible to think of Justice Kagan without ever so slightly wondering about her true sexual nature. This is what is so insidious about gossip of this kind, its propensity for muddying waters. In its online version, of course, such gossip travels faster and farther than in any other form. In an earlier time, no serious newspaper, no respectable television channel or radio station, would have asked about a Supreme Court nominee's sex life. Such dreck would have been left to the gutter press to dangle for the delectation of the low-minded. Some things might be thought but are still better left unsaid. No longer. Not in cyberspace, which, like a dirty mind, never sleeps.

Until the invention and widespread use of the Internet, gossip could be conveniently divided between private and public spheres, as it for the most part has been in the first two parts of this book. But like the distinction between gossip and news, that between the private and the public has become decisively blurred. Private gossip is largely restricted to include friends (and enemies) and acquaintances, while public gossip is about people in public life who appear in print or on radio or television, broadcast for the titillation of the larger world. To qualify for public gossip, one had to have achieved some measure of fame or notoriety. But with the advent of the Internet, one can arrive at notoriety without having first achieved anything.

"The Internet," writes Daniel J. Solove, a legal scholar interested in the questions, problems, and issues of privacy, "is transforming the nature and effects of gossip." In his book *The Future of Reputation: Gossip, Rumor, and Privacy on the Internet,* Solove recounts some of the ways this is so. He tells the story of an insensitive remark that appeared online, supposedly spoken by the clothing designer Tommy Hilfiger: "If I had known that African Americans, Hispanics, and Asians would buy my clothes, I would not have made them so nice." Hilfiger is also supposed to have confirmed that he made this most impolitic remark on *Oprah,* causing Ms. Winfrey to throw him off her show and tell her audience not to buy his clothes. The effect of this caused Hilfiger's business to slump drastically. The problem is that Tommy Hilfiger never made the remark, nor had he ever appeared on *Oprah.* But the story was out there in cyberspace; you will find it is still out there today.

Professor Solove tells many such stories. There's the woman whose name came up on the Internet as the alleged rape victim of Kobe Bryant. She wasn't in fact the victim, just the object of speculation of some ill-informed blogger. Her name remains on the Internet as a rape victim, there for her future husband and everyone else to contemplate.

Solove tells the story of a girl in South Korea who refused to clean up after her dog on a subway. A fellow rider with a cellphone camera caught her in the act of refusal and passed it along to someone else, who put it on his blog. A man with a much more popular blog picked it up and put it on his site, and from there it took off, so that the girl became known around the world as the "dog-poop girl." She was henceforth harassed, as was her family, and because of it she eventually decided it would be best to drop out of the university she attended. The moral here isn't that you should always clean up after your dog, even though you should, but that you never know who's watching, and if it's the wrong person and he has a phone camera and a friend with a blog, it can mean serious trouble.

Not long ago in the Style section of the Sunday *New York Times*, a young woman wrote a letter to an advice columnist saying that she recently broke up with her boyfriend, who has written about the breakup in his blog in a way that makes her look bad. The problem is, as she notes, if a prospective employer decides to search for her name on Google and discovers all the terrible things her ex-boyfriend has said about her, it could—more than could, it is likely to—be damaging to her chances of getting the job, not to speak of getting future boyfriends.

The Internet has been splendid in the freedom it has given people to express their opinions, in catching out politicians in egregious lies and journalists in shoddy practice, and in so much else. This immense freedom of the Internet is part of its glory. Freedom has allowed it to be iconoclastic, aiding young entrepreneurs with new ideas in design and for daily living, allowing performing artists to display their talent without constraint on YouTube, unaffiliated thinkers to express their ideas, ordinary people to express themselves, protesting citizens to overthrow dictatorships. No one would wish to take that away.

But it is the other side of that freedom—the freedom to libel, to invade privacy, to wreck lives—that has got so little, though greatly needed, attention. Professor Solove remarks that the Internet is, historically, in its adolescence—and it is precisely as an adolescent that it now tends to act: wildly, thoughtlessly, destructively. Lars Nelson, of the *New York Daily News,* has called the Internet, in this aspect of its young career, "a vanity press for the demented," and this is more than an amusing phrase.

The chief instruments of this destruction are Facebook, Twitter, and above all the blog, a name that derives from weblog, and its ally, the link. No one knows how many million blogs now exist, nor how many fresh postings—or new entries—are sent out each day. While many blogs are, as we have seen, narrowly specialized in their interests, the majority tend to be personal diaries made public. That people are willing to expose their private thoughts and feelings to the scrutiny of strangers is a sign of how radically personal notions of privacy have changed. The problem is that in many blogs, so much of what used to go into diaries can now, when served up online for anyone who cares to read them, do real damage to other people. Sometimes feelings get hurt; not infrequently much more is at stake.

Solove tells of a young woman working in the office of a U.S. senator who published a blog in which she blithely set out the details of her sex life. Her activity was frequent, and the details she supplied were copious, including the oddities of the appetites of the men with whom she bedded down. This man preferred only anal sex, that one had a taste for spanking, another gave her money for sex—that sort of thing. Soon enough her blog, originally meant only for a few of her friends, was picked up by a Beltway blog called Wonkette, itself known for its bawdiness, which had a larger following, and presently the young woman's name and the details of her sex life were broadcast much more widely than she claims at first she intended.

The strangeness of the story is that the young woman didn't seem to mind the publicity. She rather liked the notoriety it brought her. "Public embarrassment," she wrote, "is really very liberating. You really stop caring about what people think, which is something only the elderly seem to be able to accomplish with great aplomb. So I am way ahead of everybody. And those of you behind me can kiss my ass."

Some of the men she wrote about felt much less at ease with public embarrassment than she, and at least one, who argued that he was readily identifiable in her blog, sued her for invasion of privacy, claiming "severe emotional distress, humiliation, embarrassment, and anguish." Hard cheese on him, as the English say. The young woman, whose name is Jessica Cutler, flourished, at least as we understand flourishing in contemporary life. She was interviewed and photographed naked by *Playboy;* she wrote a novel called *Washingtonienne* (the name of her blog), for which she is said to have been given a $300,000 advance; and she eventually married a bankruptcy lawyer with whom she has had a daughter. No business like blog business, at least for some.

I am glad to have ceased teaching in a university before the Internet culture got going in a big-time way — before, that is, students had blogs in which, under proper disguise, they could say cruel things about one's teaching or dress or character. Let them think cruel things, or anything else for that matter, but to have it online, as part of the permanent public record, is not so much daunting as saddening — at least it would have been to me.

Two incidents: In a writing course I taught many years ago, a student, a young woman suffering from depression, on the last day of the course launched into an attack on me for favoring the would-be fiction writers in the class over the would-be poets, of whom she was one. I had no notion of doing so, and in fact hadn't a very clear idea which students wanted to be novelists and which poets. The young woman's tirade spoiled the final day of the class, and when it was over a number of students in the course came to apologize for her and to thank me for my efforts over the quarter, which touched me. This, as I say, was before the era of blogs. Today, with a blog at her disposal, the depressed young woman could have done my reputation as a teacher real damage, by posting her delusional views of me on her blog.

In another course I taught, this one on Willa Cather, a young woman told a friend who was going out with a graduate student with whom I was friendly that I favored male over female students in the class. She based this on my calling on more male than female students during discussion sessions. In truth, I would have been delighted to call on a hermaphroditic armadillo if I thought it had an intelligent contribution to make to class discussion. (It depressed me to think of a young woman, whose parents were spending more than $40,000 a year on her education, sitting there counting the number of males and females on whom her teacher was calling.) Again, I am thankful that this occurred before the age of the blog, or I would also have been saddled with the reputation of a misogynist. The combination of the Internet and political correctness is a powerful force for . . . I am not sure what, but am fairly certain it isn't the truth.

Malice, as we have seen, is also too often an element of gossip, and the Internet, in this connection, can be a powerful aid to malice, by spreading falsehoods—or even harmful truths—with a speed undreamed of by small-town over-the-back-fence gossips. Sometimes not even malice is required for the Internet to do its job as an engine for gossip. Things are mentioned on one blog, picked up by another, linked by a third to two others, and soon something meant to be strictly intramural becomes global.

Professor Solove tells of a college student, pressed for time, who asked someone who specialized in a certain subject to write a class paper for her. The man, feeling her request morally objectionable, nonetheless agreed to do so, putting into the paper all sorts of obvious errors, thinking it would bring down her grade, and then he sent an e-mail to the dean of her college informing him of what he had done. While at it, he posted on his blog that the student, whom he named, was a plagiarist. More people picked up on his blog posting than he expected, and soon the student was the subject of wide interest on the Internet, with lots of strangers writing condemnatory responses about her behavior. Suddenly people began calling her school and home, to go on record about what a wretched person she was. Meanwhile, the man who started it all wanted to call a halt; things, he felt, had got well out of hand. He wanted the young woman exposed, but not publicly pilloried. "I was faced with all of you people looking for blood," he wrote on his blog. "I didn't want blood. What I wanted was irony." The young woman was of course wrong, but did she deserve so widespread a shaming as the blogosphere here provided?

Earlier I wrote about the wide-ranging effects of gossip, its good qualities in supplying important information not available in any other form and its destructive ones when motivated by meanness and the intent to bring a person down. But on the harmful side, the Internet has quickened, and much intensified, the harm that gossip can do to its victims. Sometimes this harm is impersonal, or nearly so. The Internet, it turns out, also has a vigilante, or posse, function that is an arm of gossip. In this respect, you not only accuse a person of wrongdoing, but also join forces with others to round him up, as in the cases of the poor dog-poop girl or the student who asked someone else to write her paper.

Blogs exist, among other things, to shame people who fall below what are thought to be proper standards of behavior, in which the people who do so are named for anyone to see. I learned from Professor Solove's book that there is a blog called Bitterwaitress, which names poor tippers on what it calls the Shitty Tipper Database, or anyone who leaves tips of under fifteen, or in some cases twenty, percent of the check. The best-selling writer Malcolm Gladwell found himself named on this blog, though he claims not to recollect ever undertipping. But once his name appeared on the list, his claims counted for nothing.

Another such blog is called Don't Date Him Girl, which lists men, and their profiles, who in their relationships with women have been disloyal, sexually aggressive, liars, mama's boys, and any other information that is useful in condemning these men. All this information may be quite true—men, as I am fond of telling my granddaughter, are brutes—but what if some of it isn't? What if some of the names are placed there because a woman feels falsely betrayed or is herself psychologically off kilter or is seeking revenge for a man's not finding her attractive? In Don't Date Him Girl and other such blogs, the old question arises: Who is guarding the guardians?

Reading about these blogs, I couldn't help but wonder about taking things a step further: What about a waitress blog exposing people with atrocious table manners who eat sloppily or—worse in our era—unhealthily? Or how about adding an item to Don't Date Him Girl that comments on a man's performance in bed? Or, for that matter, establishing a Don't Date Her Guy blog that would do the same thing from the standpoint of the opposite sex?

Blogs already exist that are meaner than this. A website called

Revenge World allows the aggrieved party of a former couple to attack his or her former mate, including, in some instances, showing embarrassing photographs. People will say on the Internet things they would never say to another person face to face or over a phone. The blog, with its absence of face-to-face contact, provides something very like whiskey courage — cyber courage, let us call it — and it cannot be a good thing.

In its destructive aspect, gossip is about two things: the ruination of reputation and the invasion of privacy. No institution does these two things more efficiently than the Internet, where it can be menacing, and will remain menacing until the time when laws come into being to guard against its many excesses. Difficult even to think about the complexity of such laws, which would require guaranteeing both freedom of speech and protection of reputation and privacy. But the need for them is becoming more and more acute, as became evident when, in 2010, an eighteen-year-old student at Rutgers University, after two classmates photographed him with a webcam having sex with another male student and then put the result on Twitter, took his own life. Webcams, Twitter, the Internet, who knew such things, at the service of gossip, could be deadly instruments?

As far as I know, I have never been directly gossiped about on the Internet. I live, after all, a dullish life that does not provide much fodder for exotic gossip. But I have been insulted innumerable times online, as has anyone who writes for the general public, and insults not made to your face but with the capacity to be instantly widespread are an indirect form of gossip. I have been called a lousy writer, a reactionary, and once, honor of honors, "blowhard of the month" (December 2008, in case you missed it). Another time, someone fiddled with my Wikipedia entry, slanting my interests and the character of my career, and only through the persistent efforts of the friend who told me about it was the entry set right. But that's the Internet, where one can say anything about anyone and probably not be contradicted, even by the truth.

Stendhal said that to write a book is to risk being shot at in public. But until the Internet, one didn't know all the tender places in which one could be shot. And there is no redress, not really, not likely, not ever, not so long as the Internet remains the playground of the too often pathological and the Valhalla of the unvalorous, where the unqualified and the outright foolish can say what they please about whom they please, which in the end amounts, as Molly Haskell has it, to "democracy's revenge on democracy."

Meanwhile, until such time as laws governing behavior in cyberspace are made, or at least an etiquette for Internet behavior is developed, we are all potentially Internet victims. So clean up after your dog, never leave less than a twenty percent tip, be more than attentive and courtly on dates, do not divorce or break up with a partner . . . In fact, maybe you'd do better never to leave your apartment, what with all those little Big Brothers and Sisters out there watching you.

Diary

I have no recollection of gossip playing any part in the household in which I grew up. My parents were both intelligent, and my mother a cool and subtle judge of character, but neither seemed to hear or pass on any gossip. They might say between themselves that an acquaintance was "cheap," by which they meant unsporting in his spending; or a "four-flusher," by which they meant false in her pretensions. But there were no stories of secret drinking or adultery or truly egregious conduct. Possibly people in that time — the 1940s and early 1950s — were better at hiding their flaws. Possibly to speak ill of another person without having some foundation in fact was less tolerated. I do recall my parents scoring off an acquaintance or two for being a "busybody," but otherwise things along the gossip front were quiet.

I hope I am not making my parents sound prim, for they were not. They laughed a lot, and cut other people a fairly wide swath in their behavior. They were amused by other people's foibles and were comical about their own. But my parents, as were many of the adults of their generation, were pre-psychological; they did not attempt to explain behavior, other people's or their own, by recourse to labels put into the world by psychoanalysis and psychology. They would never say that someone behaved the way he did because he was insecure, or suffered an inferiority complex, or was paranoid, let alone that he had anything so arcane as an unresolved Oedipus complex. They looked out at the world and saw only admirable or less than admirable behavior; and under the category of unadmirable came behavior that was cowardly, dishonorable, thoughtless, ungenerous, foolish, cruel, and selfish.

As part of this pre-psychological condition, my parents were reticent, certainly about themselves. In her late seventies, my mother had liver cancer that she knew was going to end in her death. Even though her oncologist fought on against the disease, my mother, a very realistic person, in her certainty about the end of her life, was depressed, not wretchedly so, or in a way that made people around her sad, but she became less than her usual ebullient self. I happened to mention my mother's condition to a woman I know, who suggested that there were wonderful "support groups" for people suffering terminal diseases, and wondered if such a group wouldn't help my mother.

I would not for a nanosecond have thought of suggesting any such thing. Had I done so, my mother would, I have no doubt, have replied: "Let me see. You are suggesting that I go into a room full of strangers and we each tell one another our troubles and this will make me feel better. Is this what you are suggesting? Is this the kind of son I've raised, one who would suggest anything so idiotic?"

My mother's father died when she was in her adolescence. Her mother was the great matriarch of the family, loved and highly regarded by her four children. My mother rarely spoke about her father. When I quizzed her about him, which I did occasionally, and always gently, she was less than forthcoming. "He was a nice man," she would say, "a kind man." As for what he did for a living, she said that he worked in Chicago, in the garment trade. Plainly she preferred not to talk much about her father, and she, a formidable woman, was just as plainly not to be pushed to do so, even by her son.

One evening toward the end of her life, when my mother was in the hospital and my father and I were at dinner together after visiting her there, I asked him what he knew about his wife's father, whom, of course, he never met.

"He committed suicide," said my father, "but your mother doesn't know that I know. Years ago her sister Florence told me."

Now you have to understand that my mother and father were two people who, married fifty-seven years, loved each other, and without complication; each was, without the least doubt, the other's dearest and closest friend. Yet my mother felt no need to inform her husband that her father had committed suicide (I assume my grandfather must have done so out of depression, and not because of scandal of any kind), and he, my father, having come into this knowledge, never felt he ought to let her know that he knew, if only because she might not want to talk about it and the deep sadness it had to have cost her.

In fact my mother, whatever her reasons, didn't want to talk about her father's suicide, and apparently felt no overpowering need to do so. She must have viewed it as a terrible event in her life about which nothing was to be done, with no point in talking it to death. Since my mother was among the least neurotic people I have known, she was obviously living with this sadness, keeping it to herself, without any apparent distress or inner turmoil. Why talk about it? Why rehash it? What was to be gained? Nothing, evidently, that she could see. Reticence about the matter was more dignified, made more sense. And I find I love my mother all the more for her ability to live without the need to drag her sadness out into the open.

But I see that in telling this story, I am gossiping about my own mother, telling a tale she would not even now want told. What do you call a man who gossips about his own mother? At the very least, a writer, but also someone who, in regard to gossip, is not the man his mother was.

16

Whores of Information

Journalism is organized gossip.

— OSCAR WILDE

THE JOB OF THE JOURNALIST, every journalist, is to spy and to pry, to find out things that people, for various reasons, would rather not have revealed. Ordinary people spy and pry, too, at least some among us do, in the hope of getting beneath the unconvincing surface of things. But journalists earn their living spying and prying, which makes a substantial difference. They are professionals; they get paid for it; they are whores of information.

Why would anyone wish to talk to journalists, aid them in their undignified tasks? Because, the short answer is, they often have their own known, just as often unknown, motives for doing so. Manifold these motives may be. They might wish to pass along information to a journalist that would undo or short-circuit the plans of a rival or enemy. People might enjoy the brief glare of publicity journalism provides, thinking it lends significance to their lives. They might be concealing hidden (possibly devious) agendas behind such in-print identifications as "unacknowledged source," or "high-ranking Pentagon official," or "neighbor who did not wish to be identified."

Journalism was always a rough trade, not for the faint-hearted or sensitive. In *Child of the Century,* Ben Hecht recounts, during his days as a young journalist in Chicago, visiting the families of the recently deceased so that he could steal family photographs — and on one notable occasion an oil painting — so that his paper could have a likeness of the dead to accompany its obituary. Journalists have also been famously cold-blooded, a point heavily underscored in Hecht and Charles MacArthur's play *The Front Page.* The play is a caricature, but journalists have not been especially noted for their kindness or mercy. Once set out on a hot story, journalists tend not to care how many innocent parties, or civilians, get hurt.

If whores they be, no one has ever accused them of being whores with hearts of gold. And the new dispensation under which journalism operates — about which more presently — has not made them any larger-hearted or observant of people's feelings or what they hold sacred.

Of course today in public life there is no longer anything staked out as sacred, and thus inviolable to journalistic poking. Think of the publicity logjam that hit Tiger Woods when, in the winter of 2009–10, his scandal of philandering became the main item in the national news. What began as gossip about Woods turned out to be quite true — truer, or, more precisely, wilder, than anyone might have imagined. Wrong though Woods was, and deceitful into the bargain, one has to have been without imagination not to have shuddered, if only slightly, at the klieg-light glare to which his antics were exposed. He should have known better, we confidently say. He was a fraud, we all agree. Yet are we entitled to know so much about the scandal, or about the man himself, as eventually was revealed?

Some people think we are. In the *Wall Street Journal* a psychology professor named Nicholas DiFonzo, who has written a book about office gossip called *The Watercooler Effect,* is among those who do. "The Tiger gossip is replete with moral messages and motivations that are compelling, instructive and powerful," he wrote. "Moral guidance can often sound like a collection of tired bromides when expressed in the abstract. But when told as part of a compelling drama — as gossip — it can appear as an eloquent demarcation of good behavior." One wonders if DiFonzo thinks it was moral instruction that the journalists so relentless on Woods's case had in mind.

Tina Brown, the former editor of *Vanity Fair* and of *The New Yorker*, is someone else who feels that exposure through gossip can on balance be a good thing. "We live in a culture of destructive transparency," Brown wrote on her website the *Daily Beast* in connection with the leakage of a story about Mel Gibson abusing an ex-girlfriend. "Text messages leaked. Phone calls taped. Pictures uploaded in real time, and sound bites exploding on unsuspecting careers. But there's an upside to our leaky, sneaky world. Vile, fraudulent bullies like Mel Gibson or free-range sex addicts like Tiger Woods can be exposed at last to the censure — and ridicule — they deserve."

Athletes of earlier days never underwent such intense scrutiny as did Woods. The antics of Babe Ruth with women, though much talked about in a sub-rosa way, were never the stuff of the daily, even the tabloid, press. The great tennis champion Bill Tilden's homosexuality, also known to people inside the sport of tennis, was blunted, though he was charged with "lewd and lascivious behavior with a minor" and served a seven-month prison sentence for such conduct. The private life of athletes was pretty much their own. I remember as a boy reading, in *Sport* magazine, an article about Yogi Berra, the great Yankee catcher, that included the following sentence, which has stuck in my mind all these years: "Yogi enjoys plenty of pizza in the off-season, when he can usually be found at his pal Phil Rizzuto's bowling alley." Nothing more in the article was said about Yogi's private life, which was considered either of no interest or nobody's business.

No longer. *TMZ*, the celebrity gossip television show, having made great hay with its coverage of the Tiger Woods story, has recently begun a sports blog, TMZsports.com, dedicated to pursuing the delinquencies of athletes, of which, one may be sure, there will be no shortage. How could it be otherwise when you have a large number of undereducated young men, unused to people saying no to them, earning vast sums of money, out on the loose. Bad behavior of all sorts can be the only result. And with *TMZ* offering money for tips to such stories, the stories themselves are likely to come flooding in, about wife beating, gun toting, illegitimate children, minor crimes, major breaches of decorum and decency. It promises to be a field day, on a field athletes have not hitherto been asked to play.

Are celebrities—in sports, show business, politics—by the very nature of their celebrity, not entitled to the least privacy? Apparently not if caught out at bad behavior. The press used to talk about the public's right to know. But does this right extend to details, really quite grubby if not positively lurid details? Is it not enough to know that a man committed adultery? Do we also need to know he did so with a woman with a tramp stamp above her behind, her bra size, and that together they did this, that, and the other no fewer than three times while Rolling Stones music played on the hotel room stereo? Doesn't more and more exposure of this kind, in its cumulative effect, lower the tone of the society in which it takes place?

The change of social tone was a slow one, an accumulation of many bridges being lowered, gates opened, walls allowed to crumble. When was the first time an athlete said "pissed off" or "kick ass" on television, a woman said "fuck" at a middle-class dinner party table, kids took to using the phrase "it sucks" for things they didn't like, permission given to run ads for Viagra and other erection-inducing pills on prime-time television? When was the first time that older people deciding to live together without marrying, lest marriage reduce their Social Security checks, became respectable; the first time a comedian (Robin Williams?) did skits about cunnilingus on cable television; the first time *The New Yorker* permitted the word "bullshit" in its pages, with phrases such as "cunty fingers" (thank you, John Updike) in its fiction;

the first time a politician, his timorous wife by his side, publicly apologized for having been caught out at having sex with another woman or young man?

All these undated events of the past three or so decades have helped to bring down the decorum that was a strong feature of—let us call it—square society. Not many people around today to defend square society, with all its rules and inhibitions. Square society could be stuffy, boring, dreary. Not many laughs there, and no titillation whatsoever. Yet in regard to gossip, it could be much subtler than the blatant exposure that has come to pervade contemporary life. In a John O'Hara story called "The General," published in his book *Waiting for Winter* (1966), O'Hara has a retired army officer return home to find his wife, Sophie, and her female friends gathered for afternoon tea. He assumes that these women had been gossiping before his arrival from his club.

> Any real gossip Sophie had picked up would be duly passed on to him when they were alone, in language of the utmost purity but with illustrative gestures, and as completely descriptive as a police report. He had never asked her how her women friends were able to communicate details without using the language of the gutter or of the physicians; they would not repeat naughty words, and they were ignorant of medical terminology. Nevertheless Sophie and her friends made their stories graphically real, and there was nothing in the calendar of sin that she had not at some time been able to convey to him in the telling of an episode.

The decorum of square society established with some clarity what was permissible, what could and could not be said in public and, as the O'Hara story conveys, in private. If square society had a standard, it found it in the realm of taste. People of good taste simply did not do, say, or even think certain things.

One did of course think untasteful things, and in the privacy of one's home, or the intimacy of one's closest friendships, one also said tasteless things. But they weren't printed, at least not in such erstwhile respectable places as the *New York Times, The New Yorker, Vanity Fair, New York,* and elsewhere. Nor were they shown on television or said in mixed company. It took decades—one of these decades, that of the 1960s, was especially significant in this regard—for the old standards of decorum to be set aside. The increased brashness of gossip columns helped. So, too, did the changed relationships between men and women, so that things once permitted to be talked about only in exclusively male company now made it to the dinner-party table. The breakdown of censorship in literature, once one of the great and worthy causes of liberalism, brought with it the dreary consequences of adult bookstores and easy access to pornography on the Internet. For many people the defeat of decorum and the rise of candor represents pure progress. Others, toting up the side effects, are not so sure.

The New Yorker is in some ways a good gauge of the change in social arrangements that has paved the way for public discussion of things once thought best discussed, if at all, in private. In its pages, under an earlier editor, William Shawn, no profane language was permitted, nor was fiction that included the description of sex allowed. Until Shawn's enforced retirement in 1987, at the age of eighty, if one saw a story by John Cheever or John Updike published elsewhere than in *The New Yorker,* one could be sure that sex was going to be described in it. Was Shawn a prude? Whether he was or not is perhaps up for argument, but what isn't is the fact that he was a great editor, perhaps the greatest magazine editor of the past century. His good taste—or, if you prefer, his puritanism—in matters of language and risqué subject matter didn't seem to get in the way of that; it may even have had something to do with his greatness.

After William Shawn died, in 1992, Lillian Ross, a longtime reporter at *The New Yorker,* wrote a memoir in which she described her decades-long love affair with the married Mr. Shawn. *Here but Not Here* (1998) the memoir is called, and it was published while Cecille Shawn, Shawn's wife, was still alive. Before Lillian Ross's book, William Shawn was a figure of mystery, elusive, self-effacing to the point of near nonexistence.

Except that he distinctly did exist, and no single man or woman over the past fifty or so years had more books dedicated to him by grateful writers or was featured so emphatically in authors' acknowledgments. Had he his druthers, Shawn would probably have preferred that all these writers allow him to go without mention. He claimed not to like to see his name in print, and there is no reason to disbelieve him. This was a man who turned down honorary degrees from, among other places, Harvard, Yale, Princeton, Cornell, Columbia, and Michigan; he had attended the last-named school for two years before dropping out. Shawn was also a man with lots of phobias—he refused to fly in a plane, he panicked in elevators and crowds, he couldn't bear smoke, alcohol made him nervous, fast cars made him anxious, he was always cold, even in warmest summer—and this is merely the icing on a rich cake of his neuroses.

If Lillian Ross's account is to be believed, William Shawn would have been happier never to have been the editor of *The New Yorker* in the first place. What he really wanted to be was a writer. Working so closely with and on behalf of other writers cost him, Miss Ross tells us, the sense of "his own existence." His marriage brought him no happiness, either; nor, one gathers, did his being the father of three children, one of them a twin girl who is deeply autistic. All this, of course, according to Lillian Ross. If Shawn was self-effacing, Ross is self-aggrandizing, certainly in her privacy-destroying memoir *Here but Not Here,* a title that comes from Shawn's frequently telling her that, when in his marital home, he was "there but not there." That, when she first read it—and one hopes she never did—could not have come as cheering news to Mrs. Shawn.

Lillian Ross, through her gossipy book, has what we today would call "demystified" one of the last century's most interestingly mysterious cultural figures. She has done so by rendering him, as a photograph of Shawn on page 127 of her book displays him, rather a sad, schlumpy little man, a bag of needs and frustrations encased in a dark, vested suit, a pathetic cloth cap atop his large bald head.

Several reasons for why she would do this to a man she professes to have loved might be adduced, but the background reason is surely that the times permit it, one might even say encourage it. Lillian Ross had an experience of some intensity with a man famous for not being famous, and she felt no obligation to keep it to herself but instead preferred to advertise it to the world, no matter what damage it might have done to William Shawn's family or to the reputation of the man himself.

Hard to know how aware Lillian Ross is of the extent of that damage. She prides herself on being a pure type of reporter, leaving herself out of her writing, most of which has over the decades appeared in *The New Yorker.* But it was Lillian Ross who also destroyed the reputation of Ernest Hemingway, in a *New Yorker* profile, by making him look a buffoon, filled with himself and without the least self-knowledge. "I started out quiet and then I beat Mr. Turgenev," Hemingway declares at one point during his interview. "Then I trained hard and I beat Mr. de Maupassant. I fought two draws with Mr. Stendhal, and I think I had an edge in the last one. But nobody's going to get me in the ring with Mr. Tolstoy, unless I'm crazy or I keep getting better." Although Lillian Ross seems to have had no sense of it, after Hemingway opened himself up in front of her, and she wrote and published his foolish pronouncements, it was no longer possible to take him quite seriously as a writer. In her *New Yorker* profile, she killed Ernest Hemingway more surely than any critic could have done.

The problem is not over Lillian Ross's having had an affair with William Shawn, or over his affair with her, but with her need to publicize the details while injured parties were still alive. "After forty years," she writes, "our love-making had the same passion, the same energies (alarming to me, at first), . . . the same tenderness, the same inventiveness, the same humor, the same textures as it had in the beginning. It never deteriorated, our later wrinkles, blotches, and scars of age notwithstanding." Shawn, who made not hurting the feelings of others one of his first principles, could not have been other than appalled and deeply ashamed had he read his inamorata's book.

Fifty years ago, Lillian Ross would not have written such a book. If she had, no one would have published it. If against all odds she could have found someone to publish it, reviewers would have demolished it. But now, how different the atmosphere and appetite for such revealing gossip is. Now she, as a reporter, could scarcely hold such a story back. Or so she must have felt. What she seems not to have noticed is that in her book she makes her dearest love out to be a pathetic neurotic and a monster of selfish cruelty.

Candor has been greatly, perhaps too greatly, heightened in our day. With the stakes of candor everywhere raised, the premium is on the new and edgy. People who write autobiographies or memoirs must have something at least slightly shocking—better of course if it is powerfully shocking—to convey. A writer named Michael Greenberg languishes in relative obscurity until he decides to write a memoir of the nightmare of living with his daughter's manic episodes. But shouldn't it be the daughter's memoir to write, if written it must be? Fiction, to be talked about, now requires a jolt of the wildly unexpected, such as that of a short story in *The New Yorker* some years ago about a young woman who is planning *in vitro* fertilization and imagines a bouillabaisse of semen whose contributors include various males whose discrete good qualities—physical, mental, psychological—will go into the making of her child. People who go on talk shows must leap the obstacles of decorum to say something outré; charm alone will no longer suffice.

Gossip, too, has felt the need to become heightened in intensity, wilder, more revealing. "Been there, done that," a phrase that suggests boredom and impatience, is also one of the most damning to hear for anyone hoping to bring something either professionally or privately entertaining to an audience of readers, or even of friends. In an age when it's allowed openly to discuss the sexual appetite and habits of a man who held his privacy dear above all else, anything goes.

Diary

I have not often been in possession of information that journalists were eager to have. One occasion when I did was while I was a member of the National Council of the National Endowment for the Arts, at a time when everything about the Endowment seemed to be in the high flux of controversy. A serious scandal had hit the NEA over the revelation that it had given out grants in connection with such works of putative art as a bottle of urine that also contained a crucifix; photographs that would appear to qualify as obscene, one of which was of a man with a toilet plunger up his rectum; performance artists who smeared chocolate or blood over their bodies; and more such assaultive art. All sorts of interesting questions arose: Should the government sponsor art meant to scandalize? Should taxpayers be asked to pay for it? Shouldn't artists with a taste for *épater*-ing the establishment do so on their own nickel? The NEA and the National Council were torn by such questions, Congress was threatening to cut off funding, artists' groups were outraged at the possible abrogation of artistic freedom — and the debate over these matters was considered fairly high-priority news. All this was made more piquant by the fact that a number of famous artists served on the council: Martha Graham, Robert Joffrey, Celeste Holm, Robert Stack, and others. The questions, moreover, did not allow for neutral answers. Everyone, in and out of the council, myself included, was *parti pris*.

For the first and only time in my life, then, I began to get calls from reporters, hoping that I could give them some potent insiderish information — read: gossip — on what was going on at the NEA during these wild times. Because I thought I could say a thing or two to clarify the debate, I responded to a request for an interview from the *New York Times* reporter Richard Bernstein, whom I knew to be honest and honorable. Bernstein promised to show me not his finished article but any quotations of mine he planned to use in it before the paper went to press, and he did so. The result was entirely satisfactory: the article was fair, I was allowed to make my points, and an aura of seriousness prevailed.

My views set out in the *Times* piece didn't stop other journalists from wanting more from me—on the contrary, it probably encouraged them. I put them all off, politely enough, I hope, by telling them that everything I had to say on the subject I had said to Richard Bernstein. All, that is, but a reporter from the *Boston Globe,* whose name I am pleased to have forgotten, who insisted that I had an obligation to supply him with more information of a clearly gossipy kind. I said I didn't feel any obligation to do so. "But what about the public's right to know?" he asked. "The public," I said, exasperated by the fellow's persistence. "Of course, I forgot the dear public. Next time you see the public, please tell it to go stick it in its ear," and I hung up.

17

Snoopin' and Scoopin'

The first step in good reporting is good snooping.

— MATT DRUDGE

E VERYONE KNOWS THAT politicians have been, and continue to be, great subjects for gossip. The Kennedy family has long been a cottage industry of gossip unto itself: all that free-floating fornication, drunkenness, drug abuse, uninvestigated manslaughter, and the rest. Some of the scandalous — which is also to say gossip-worthy — behavior of politicians was in the past concealed by their ability to bring the press onto their side. No longer, given the prevailing atmosphere of the day, can such arrangements be made.

What is perhaps less well known is the role that gossip plays in the mechanics of politics — its role, that is, in the everyday life of getting deals done or killed, ending electoral hopes, or forcing retirements from public life. I refer to leaks, which are little more than gossip turned to the service and ends of politics. Any historian of American politics of the past fifty or so years who does not take leaks into account is missing a significant part of the motor force of recent American history. So prevalent have leaks become as a way of doing politics that the day may come when we have a

Secretary of Leaks, whose job will be plugging, controlling, initi-ating, and directing the intense traffic of it all.

Is a political leak actually gossip? What if the leak is true? What if it is used for a good cause? Are such leaks still gossip? Best to re-member our root definition of gossip as one party telling another what a third party doesn't want known. A political leak qualifies here. Best to remember, too, that gossip may well be true; and it frequently is true, and is often most destructive when true. Much better, for example, to be accused, in gossip, of adultery one didn't commit than of adultery one has in fact committed. Truth, therefore, does not destroy gossip but often only increases its po-tency. Not all but much gossip has the tincture of betrayal. And so do many leaks. A leak represents a disloyalty, if not to those people whom the leak will damage, to whom no loyalty may be owed or felt, but often to the code connected with the job one holds that put one in possession of the leaked material to begin with.

Many people may feel that "Deep Throat," the man who leaked the key information about Watergate to Bob Woodward and Carl Bernstein, did a great service to his country, which he may well have done. But in order to do it, he — and we now know that the man was William Mark Felt Sr., a senior FBI official — had to betray his agency's rule not to leak the information in his pos-session, about the men who broke into the Democratic National Committee's office at the Watergate complex, which ultimately resulted in President Richard Nixon's resignation.

Such is the frequency of leaked information in government that there is, as I write, a piece of legislation before Congress called the Free Flow of Information Act, designed to give journal-ists protection from the law in not having to reveal the names of the sources of information leaked to them. Critics of the legisla-tion claim that it makes political business by leak easier than it already is. Certainly leaks in politics come under the heading of business as usual, or at least have for a long while. Not only are leaks used to help bring down governments — as Deep Throat's leaks did — but they make it much more difficult for the administration in power to carry on business. But, then, administrations in power have themselves been known to leak information that will help disqualify their opponents, or help push forward their own plans and programs.

Leaks, then, are often little more than well-aimed gossip in political dress. They may always have played a limited role in government, but they came into their own with the advent and rise of investigative journalism. Investigative journalism itself ascended to the level of heroism with Woodward and Bernstein's work exposing Watergate. So much of investigative journalism in the years immediately following their triumph—a best-selling book and commercially successful movie being among the reporters' trophies—had to do with the cultivation of leaks by journalists.

The question to ask about men and women who initiate leaks, as it is with those who initiate any gossip, is, What's in it for them? Why would a person in possession of ostensibly secret information wish to convey it to a journalist? The motives range from genuine idealism to ugly revenge, with a multiplicity of possible motives in between. Often intense bureaucratic rivalries cause one faction to leak information that will make life difficult for an opposing faction in the same agency or department. One of the differences between leaks and much gossip is that gossip can be merely for entertainment; leaks are always made with a purpose—to bring down or raise up someone in politics or to foil or advance some political plan or party. The relationship between the person providing the leak and the person disseminating it, the journalist, is usually corrupt on both sides; unlike the case of standard gossip, with leaks there are no innocent bystanders or a merely mildly amused audience.

Seymour Hersh, who has worked for the *New York Times* and *The New Yorker* and has won a Pulitzer Prize for exposing the murder of civilians in the village of My Lai by American troops during the Vietnam War, is a journalist who has lived off leaks—who without the benefit of leakers might just be out of business. His professional life has been based on the anonymous source. He cultivates sources—that is, people in proximity to power, or formerly in power, who for one reason or another have gone sour or disagree emphatically with current government policy; their sourness or disagreement makes them susceptible to ratting out the people with whom they disagree or simply don't like.

Hersh's work, most recently in *The New Yorker*, is studded with comments made by a "high-ranking Pentagon official," "former CIA agent," "administration insider," "retired State Department strategist," and more of the same. The editor of *The New Yorker* is said to have the actual names of these mystery men who constitute Hersh's sources, but that isn't quite enough to make his brokering of leaks entirely persuasive. (When I read him, to relieve the tedium of all these unnamed sources, I put in their place characters of my own: "disgruntled former wife," "heavily tattooed disowned son," "deeply disappointed mother," "meshuggeneh aunt"; the comic relief, I find, helps.) Like any good gossip, Hersh prefers dramatic over staid stories. A good Hersh piece might have the U.S. government secretly financing an Arab terrorist group out of Henry Kissinger's Swiss bank account.

An additional problem is that Seymour Hersh has a locked-in set of political views. They are left wing, welcoming to all conspiracy theories that make the American government in power look devious, skeptical only of the possibility of honorable motives, rarely considering that untoward events in politics are sometimes owing to simple ineptitude. This makes the leaks he retails seem rather prefabricated. Hersh stories, whatever their subject, have essentially the same theme: the sons of bitches are up to no good.

Bob Woodward, who, after his reporting days with Carl Bernstein went on to write his own books, has a far less obvious political slant than Hersh. I am less than certain of Woodward's politics; forced to guess, I would describe them as centrist, somewhat liberal. But Woodward is himself so nearly a man of the establishment, no matter which party is in power, that his leak-brokering scarcely has the element of mischievousness and malice that much stirring gossip has. But in the end, gossip it, too, is.

Woodward comes across as a reporter with serious connections conveying just the facts, ma'am. Yet his books, invariably bestsellers, made so by political and news junkies, have the cachet they do chiefly because he is able to obtain lengthy interviews with major political players. No "top-ranking CIA agent" or "senior Pentagon official" for Bob Woodward; he deals directly with secretaries of state, defense, treasury, vice presidents, Supreme Court justices, and the president himself, whoever he happens to be at the time.

Why they choose to talk with Woodward is fairly clear. What he is writing in his books is taken to be a form of contemporary history, and men and women in power do not wish to be painted as being on the wrong side, raising Woodward's ire by refusing to talk with him. He also offers them an excellent chance to state their own positions, which can sometimes entail undermining the positions of others. So a recently resigned secretary of state might tell Woodward that he was hoodwinked or blindsided by other cabinet members with hidden agendas in connection with, say, sending American troops to Iraq. A Supreme Court justice might take the occasion of a lengthy Woodward interview to unburden himself of subtle criticism of his fellow justices. These moments of revelation, of elevated gossip, are what eager readers look for in Bob Woodward's books, and he rarely fails to supply it.

The question of leaks has been made much more complicated, as has all the world of information, by the advent of the Internet, where leaks can threaten the security of nations. As it has with gossip generally, the Internet has raised the stakes of the political gossip that goes by the name of leaks. In 2009 a supposedly disaffected intelligence analyst named Bradley Manning leaked a video to a website called WikiLeaks showing an American raid on an Afghan village in which 140 civilians, women and children included, may have been killed. The raid really happened; an unknown yet far from small number of innocent people perished. The U.S. Army would never have released such a video, for the sensible reason that it could only lower the morale of American and other troops fighting against the Taliban in Afghanistan. The leaker turned out to be a man said to have been under pressure as a homosexual under the military's "don't ask, don't tell" rule, and with a grievance against the army for demoting him in rank for assaulting another soldier. But the larger point is that the Internet, through the higher gossip of political leaks, makes possible a wide audience for anyone with a grievance in possession of classified information. And now, as we have come to know more about WikiLeaks and its head, Julian Assange, we begin to realize the serious, even deadly, consequences political leaks can have.

Perhaps the archperformer in the realm of political gossip and leaks has been Matt Drudge. Drudge's politics are libertarian-conservative. He prides himself on having been an uninterested student, a college dropout who went on to become a clerk at a Hollywood 7-Eleven and later at a CBS souvenir shop. In the latter job he kept on the qui vive for gossip, mainly about television and show business. As he told the story himself, in a talk to the National Press Club in 1998: "Overhearing, listening to careful conversations, intercepting the occasional memo—[I] would volunteer in the mail room from time to time—I hit pay dirt when I discovered that the trash cans in the Xerox room at Television City were stuffed each morning with overnight Nielsen ratings—information gold. I don't know what I did with it . . . Me and my friends knew *Dallas* had got a 35-share over *Falcon Crest*. But we thought we were plugged in."

On a computer his father bought him, Drudge began sending out his scraps of such gossip to friends via e-mail. He broke the story that Jerry Seinfeld wanted a million dollars per episode for the *Seinfeld* show. His e-mail list grew; others wanted to be on it. He began to send it out under the name *The Drudge Report*. Soon he was sending thousands of e-mails, and so he set up a website. He extended the range of his gossip from Hollywood to Washington, the city of his birth. He broke the story about Bill Clinton's antics with Monica Lewinsky; he did so by reporting that *Newsweek* had such a story ready to run but at the last moment decided against going ahead with it. When the mainstream media decide to act responsibly, freebooters such as Drudge are always ready to step in and do the dirty work. Drudge soon became more interested in politics than in show business, though he tended to treat both alike. (After all, what is Washington, as has been said, but Hollywood for homely people?) Politics, show biz, to Drudge it's all the same—snooping and scooping.

His snooping and scooping has made Matt Drudge a nice living; some say more than a million dollars a year. Drudge sees himself as more than merely lucky, or being rewarded for hard work. He views himself as part of a trend, a movement, an irresistible wave—a tsunami is more like it. "What's going on here?" he asked in his National Press Club talk:

> Well, clearly there is a hunger for unedited information, absent corporate considerations. As the first guy who has made a name for himself on the Internet, I've been invited to more and more high-toned gatherings such as this, the last being a conference on Internet & Society and some word I couldn't pronounce, up at Harvard a week ago. And I mention this not just to blow my own horn, but to make a point. Exalted minds—the panelists' and the audience's average IQ exceeds the Dow Jones—didn't appear to have a clue what this Internet's going to do; what we're going to make of it, what we're going to—what this is all going to turn into. But I have glimpses . . .
>
> We have entered an era vibrating with the din of small voices. Every citizen can be a reporter, can take on the powers that be. The difference between the Internet, television and radio, magazines, newspapers is the two-way communication. The Net gives as much voice to a 13-year-old computer geek like me as to a CEO or speaker of the House. We all become equal. And you would be amazed what the ordinary guy knows.

Ah yes, that vibrating din of small voices. It will soon, if it hasn't already, replace the boom of larger voices: the shrill sounds of the Walter Winchells, Leonard Lyonses, Dorothy Kilgallens, and Liz Smiths, even those who attempt to replace them on *TMZ* and Page Six, not to speak of the aspiring investigative reporters at the *New York Times,* the *Washington Post,* the *Chicago Tribune,* the *Los Angeles Times,* and lesser papers. Nobody, including Matt Drudge, knows for certain, but it is beginning to look as if that vibrating din of small voices will one day make the information whores of old seem like upstanding Boston virgins.

"Unedited information," Matt Drudge calls it. Perhaps those two words might stand in as another definition of gossip. Whence derives this strong appetite for the unedited information now flooding the world? Just possibly from the fact that edited information—that is, information thoroughly checked, put through a filter of thoughtful discretion about its consequences, then re-checked—is simply too boring for a culture more and more attuned to the quick, the half-read, the incomplete. Unedited information serves as the hors d'oeuvre for grazing for the not deeply interested but merely curious generations brought up with computer information. This same culture, our culture, has become one of distractions, and gossip is nothing if not distracting.

Seymour Hersh, Bob Woodward, Politico.com, and other of the investigative journalists and journalistic institutions of our day might be miffed—more than miffed, ticked to the max—to learn that they are mainly purveyors of gossip. Calling them such puts a dent in their pretensions, but not in those of Matt Drudge, who is without any pretensions whatsoever, but knows that gossip is what pays, especially gossip dressed up to look significant.

Diary

Not long after Tina Brown was appointed editor of *The New Yorker,* following a publicity-stirring if not financially successful run as editor of *Vanity Fair,* I was asked by the *London Times Literary Supplement* to write a review of a book by the old-line *New Yorker* writer Joseph Mitchell. In the course of doing so, I noted that the times had so changed that the subjects Mitchell wrote best about—odd but fascinating unknown characters in and about New York—were no longer around, and even if they were, the magazine, under its current editorship, would have no room for Mitchell's interest in the merely delightfully unusual and idiosyncratic, but was solely interested in the celebrated and infamous. I went on to compare Tina Brown's *New Yorker* to "an elegant old friend who had discovered a novelty store on the way home from work and had taken to leaving plaster-of-paris dog droppings and rubber vomit on one's carpeting." A fairly rough insult, or so I thought at the time. I find it difficult to imagine that Brown did not see these words. Yet not much later I was invited, by one of her subeditors, to write for *The New Yorker*, and it was only under her editorship that my writing appeared there with any regularity. This woman, I concluded, is more complicated than I had thought.

Ms. Zeitgeist

Lady Evans, she is, CBE (Commander of the Order of the British Empire), if you can fancy that, dearie. But she will always be Tina to me, rather like the Miss Brown in the song Billie Holiday sang, the one about "lovable, huggable Emily Brown, Miss Brown to you." Except that Tina Brown, one of the great editorial entrepreneurs of our time and a *maestra* of modern gossip, is Tina not to me alone but to hundreds of thousands, perhaps millions of people through creating her own insiderly, buzzy, gossipy journalism.

An editorial genius of a kind, her strength in this line could not have been employed had Tina Brown not also possessed many skills in the art of self-advancement. But all this would be as nothing if it had not been accompanied by her strong sense of what people want to know and her ability to produce it. What they want to know, according to the Gospel of Tina, is the lowdown on the rich and famous, the powerful and the beautiful, but they want it without feeling themselves in the least *National Enquirer* lower class. Tina's skill is to make essentially debased interest, misplaced curiosity, and voyeuristic emotion seem not tacky but perfectly all right, fun, smart.

Christina Brown was born in 1953, the daughter of an English movie producer named George Hambley Brown and Bettina Brown; the latter worked for the more successful movie producer Alexander Korda. From an early age Tina was surrounded by what the English call "namey" people, brought to their home through her father's work in the movies and her attractive mother's social climbing. Her mother was half-Jewish, and in the old rigid class system wasn't able to ascend very high up the social mountain. Such fantasies of advancement as she entertained she invested in her daughter.

A self-starter, the young Tina Brown was a woman who knew what she wanted and had a fairly precise notion of what it took to acquire it. She wanted above all to be an insider, rich and famous herself while reserving the right to mock the rich and famous and chronicle what life was like among those securely inside. She didn't get into a first-class women's college at Oxford, which was a setback. Still, Oxford is Oxford. As a child, Tina was pudgy and wore thick glasses. As a young woman, the pudginess turned into the zaftig; a young man she went out with at Oxford referred to her in retrospect in those days as "a blond Monica Lewinsky." Unlike Monica, she did not get to do a president or prime minister, but she apparently did all right, bonking her way up the food chain of Oxford celebrity. Another young man, mentioned in Judy Bachrach's book *Tina and Harry Come to America,* remembers her wearing sunglasses and having "a thrusting bosom" upon which, he added, she should have worn the sunglasses.

Tina had flings with young men thought to be going somewhere and with a few members of the British upper class, who were already there. At twenty, she broke up the marriage of a film director. She had a longish liaison with the writer Martin Amis, son of the novelist Kingsley Amis, who, as his son once put it, was "promiscuous at a time when it took real energy to be promiscuous." Auberon Waugh, son of the novelist Evelyn Waugh and a successful journalist of the day, was another gentleman friend, who did much to promote Tina's early journalistic talent with editors of smart English newspapers and magazines. If one can't be a bonker of true geniuses, one can at least give their sons a go.

Tina was a subtle and powerful networker well before the word "networking" had come into being. Given the least bit of a shove, Tina knew how to glide, then soar. As a working journalist, she came through with gossipy, glossy, bitchy, with-it articles comprising precisely the right combination of smartness, snobbery, and gossip. She might have had a successful career as a journalist, but must have sensed that writing, for someone with her ambition, wasn't where the action was.

Tina Brown came into the world when the English aristocracy was still in existence, envied if no longer much admired, still holding a snobbish card or two, but no longer in possession of the kind of power to squash a Becky Sharp–like career of the kind she had set upon. As a testament to the breakup of the old English class system, the man Tina married, Harold Evans, twenty-five years older than she, though working class, rose to the pinnacle of English newspaper journalism, first as editor in chief of the London *Sunday Times* and then of the *Times* itself. He was installed in the latter job, from which he would soon be humiliatingly fired, by no less than an Australian, Rupert Murdoch. Working-class editors, Australian press lords, pushy young female journalists with thrusting bosoms . . . ah, England, it long ago began to look as if there may not always be an England after all — it was, in any event, Mick Jagger's country now.

Further evidence that the old class system was breaking up was apparent in the hiring of Tina Brown to edit *Tatler,* a magazine founded in the early eighteenth century by Richard Steele, the editor, with Joseph Addison, of the *Spectator,* which in more recent years had been devoted to chronicling the social lives of what was left of the British aristocracy. Rather than continuing worshipfully to chronicle these people, Tina turned the magazine into an organ of sly mockery of them. She invited her old Oxford pals — Martin Amis, Julian Barnes, Ian McEwan, among others — to join her in the venture.

Tina remained three and a half years at *Tatler.* During this time, she raised both the circulation of the magazine and her own visibility, but did rather less for the financial health of the magazine, which lost money. This would be a repeating pattern in Tina Brown's career: she enlivens the institutions she works for, adding greatly to their circulation, and while they lose money, she gains reputation. Reputation, please note, not prestige, for prestige was not a chip at the poker game that Tina saw herself playing. "Prestige is dead," she once told someone who spoke to her of the reverence in which *The New Yorker* had long been held.

In 1983, Samuel I. Newhouse, the owner of Condé Nast magazines and, with his family, of many newspapers, acquired *Tatler.* He had earlier bought, and had plans for revamping, the old *Vanity Fair,* a slick magazine of the 1920s, edited by Frank Crowninshield, a renowned editor of his day. Newhouse had quickly run through two editors for the new *Vanity Fair*—the first, a man named Richard Locke, lasted all of three issues; the second was Leo Lerman, whom we encountered earlier and who had been a free-ranging editorial adviser for Condé Nast. A Newhouse lieutenant suggested Tina Brown for the job. The timing could not have been better. With Harry Evans a few years before fired by Rupert Murdoch from the London *Times,* and Tina beginning to grow bored with *Tatler* and its rather circumscribed readership, life in America must have seemed a smashing idea. Though only thirty-one in 1984, Tina was too savvy not to realize that, as a theater of operations for anyone with her ambition, England was now second rate, if not utterly finished. America was the place to be.

She began work at *Vanity Fair* surrounded by enemies, chiefly those who felt a lingering loyalty to Leo Lerman, whom they believed had been ditched in favor of this young English upstart. How could Newhouse put a big-budget American magazine in the hands of a woman who had no firsthand experience of the country? Tina's want of American experience would remain a criticism of her when she later took over the editorship of *The New Yorker.* What did she know of America, having seen it only from the inside of Newhouse-paid-for limousines or from the private jets or in the homes of the superwealthy of New York, Hollywood, and Washington, D.C.?

Richard Locke, during his brief tenure at *Vanity Fair,* had tried to take the magazine in a serious direction. Then Leo Lerman headed it in a metropolitan direction: sophisticated, urban, yet somehow intellectual. Tina had other ideas. She intended to bring a new element to slick-magazine journalism, to cause continual buzz and constant stir, to ride the wind of the with-it. The famous, the rich, the powerful, these were to be the subjects at the heart of *Vanity Fair* under its new British editor. Celebrity journalism is the name given to the direction in which she took the magazine.

Editing a magazine seems simple enough. An editor decides what she wants in it; she assigns writers to produce articles on these subjects; she uses other editors to get the articles in the most presentable form, with photographers and art directors to make the presentation of the articles as appealing as possible. If an editor has a good sense of the whole, of the forest in which she plants her trees, the mix of articles will make for a strong issue, something in it for everyone and lots in it for most of the magazine's regular readers.

Simple enough—but if you are Tina Brown, it is imperative that your articles cause buzz, which may be defined as the excitement of being on the inside, up to the moment, in the know, at least as voyeuristically as reading can make it. Buzz is created by discovering and writing about those people who, owing to their money, power, talent, or good looks, seem admirably, enviably well ahead of the rest of us in the always precarious game of leading the great good glamorous life. Buzz is the sizzle—hold the steak, which may or may not be served later. In the world of buzz, the names of these people are always changing: people once so of the moment suddenly seem so out of it, themselves no longer of the least moment, but dull, dreary—buzzless.

Buzz of course also assumes lots of gossip, for if buzz is the destination, gossip is usually the mode of getting there. "Insiderly," a word of Tina Brown's devising, was the quality that she was after. To know the kind of clothes significant people wear and the houses and apartments they live in and what they pay for them; to understand their psychological motivations, their romantic interests, their social calendars; to know these things, and anything else of gossipy interest about them, yet somehow not feel demeaned by one's own low curiosity—this is the trick of producing buzz.

Buzz-producing people were almost invariably celebrities, who captured the interest of the moment through their money or connections or outlandish behavior or social antecedents, or simply by their talent for attracting publicity: Leona Helmsley, Imelda Marcos, Donald Trump, Madonna, Cher, Kennedy widows and children, movie directors and stars, people known less for durable achievement than for embodying the spirit of the time, the Zeitgeist. Capturing the Zeitgeist has always been the name of Tina's desire. Madonna is perhaps a perfect example, a woman endlessly changing herself to suit the style of the moment; in fact, Tina Brown herself has been called the Madonna of contemporary journalism.

The present is the only tense Tina Brown seems ever to have known or cared to live in. What's going on, what's going down, what's happening, what buzzin'—now! Occasional pieces would appear in *Vanity Fair* about Haiti or Russia or on serious artists, but the role of these was little more than that of the Bible in the whorehouse; they weren't what brought people to the magazine. As befits a magazine devoted to the now, nothing published in it endured, nor was meant to. The only journalist whose career Tina Brown can have been said to have made is that of the photographer Annie Leibovitz. ("Annie is a Zeitgeist creature herself," Tina said.) Dominick Dunne was another *Vanity Fair* mainstay; he reported on the murder trials of the rich and famous, with plenty of room left over for name-dropping and gossip. ("The reason I'm good on assholes," Dunne averred, "is that I was once an asshole myself.")

Vanity Fair was a magazine devoted to a fantasy of the highlife. The highlife, as Tina Brown understood it, was royalty, clothing designers, movie stars, the wildly wealthy. What was on offer for readers was the illusion that one was getting a privileged peek into how these people really lived. The editor hired what today we would call networkers to sidle up to and seduce the magazine's subjects and let them expose themselves to the *Vanity Fair* treatment: elaborate photo sessions, admiring prose, hyped-up profiles, all in exchange for tidbits of gossip and an insiderly view of their lives.

If one had to select a single sentence to stand for all Tina's years as editor of *Vanity Fair,* it would be one from her own article "The Mouse That Roared," about the young Princess Diana, who was just then engaging the frivolous world's attention in a powerful way; the sentence, the article's concluding one, reads: "The debonair Prince [Charles] is pussy-whipped from here to eternity." At the sentence's final cadence one can hear the bells of Westminster Abbey gong to mark the demise of a once great country, done in by gossipy journalism.

Under Tina Brown the circulation of *Vanity Fair* continued to rise, at one point reaching more than a million readers, and in 1991 it even showed a profit. Clearly it was, as they say in the trade, the "hot book" of its day. But over the years of Tina's tenure it is estimated that *Vanity Fair* lost roughly $63 million. The reason the magazine lost so much money was because of its editor's impressive extravagance. She paid the highest salaries to steal editors from other publications; the fees she paid writers were much greater than any other magazine paid, and not infrequently she scrapped the articles they produced, doubtless for their being of insufficient sizzle. Under her editorship, the magazine had a strong publicity arm, and was known for the Gatsby-like hollow grandeur of its parties. As an editor, Tina was not about making money, not about producing literature, but about attracting attention.

Her skill in doing so clearly impressed Si Newhouse, for not long after acquiring *The New Yorker* he decided to make Tina Brown its editor. (He also installed her husband as president and editor in chief of Random House, the publishing firm.) One thing to turn a fledgling—also failing—magazine like *Vanity Fair* over to a brash journalist without any conviction apart from the importance of being up to the moment; quite another to turn over to her *The New Yorker,* that holy of holies, easily the most sacrosanct publication in twentieth-century America.

Whereas *The New Yorker* before Tina Brown was loved, while she was its editor it was talked about. Buzz, buzz, buzz. To be sure, it had been talked about before, but in a different way, having published controversial essays by Rachel Carson on pollution, Hannah Arendt on the victims of the Holocaust, and James Baldwin on the Black Muslims. But buzz, as Tina understood it, was never part of the deal on West Forty-third Street, where the magazine had had its offices for decades. Instead of buzz, the old *New Yorker,* some thought, specialized only in zzzz, running excruciatingly lengthy articles on wheat, geological faults, and other distinctly unbuzzy subjects. *New Yorker* writers were coddled, allowed to take years to turn in articles; under William Shawn's editorship, the magazine's writer on baseball, Roger Angell, would sometimes turn in his piece on the World Series in February. Sometimes it seemed as if the magazine was making a determined—and actually quite successful—effort not to be up to the moment.

Tina Brown eliminated criticism and short stories from *Vanity Fair,* and was apparently not keen to have them in *The New Yorker,* though these items were at the heart of the magazine's appeal. When she became its editor, she announced that "seriousness will be sexy again. Substance is back in style." The reaction was furious. Garrison Keillor viewed Tina Brown's ascension to the editorship of *The New Yorker* by noting: "If some ditzy American editor went to London, took over the *Spectator,* and turned it into, say, *In Your Face: A Magazine of Mucus,* there would be a big uproar. Here, a great American magazine falls into the clutches of a British editor who seems to know this country mainly from television and movies and nobody says much about it."

Keillor was one of the *New Yorker* contributors who resigned upon Tina Brown's hiring. Tina let go of some seventy-odd other writers and editors, many of whom had longtime relationships with the magazine. The tendency was to cut away—how to say it?—the less buzzy; among them were John McPhee, the excellent science writer Jeremy Bernstein, and the earnest Washington correspondent Elizabeth Drew. From *Vanity Fair* she brought over writers who knew how to deliver the kind of goods she wanted. Assuming readers had as short an attention span as she—"boring" was her ultimate putdown for writing that in her view did not come off—Tina cut the length of *New Yorker* articles, allowed the deliberately outré into its pages, and emphasized the lively over the thoughtful.

Some felt that Tina Brown saved *The New Yorker,* which was said to be on the slide into gradual decline. She certainly did what she could to shock the magazine's old-line readers. She published covers meant to outrage, such as the one in which a Hasid is kissing a black woman. She turned one issue over to the foulmouthed comedienne Roseanne Barr, an experiment that flopped. She opened the gates to rougher language and more sex-ridden stories. Daphne Merkin, a writer with a penchant for unnecessary confession, published an article on the pleasure that being spanked by men gave her. With her emphasis on Hollywood, the magazine began to feel, some thought, as if it were being edited in Los Angeles.

Tina received some praise and much criticism for her efforts as editor of *The New Yorker.* But she achieved her main object, which was to cause a stir, to be talked about. In the course of all the stir, more of Si Newhouse's money went down the tubes, vast sums of it, to pay for articles never published, issues torn up and remade at the last possible moment, galas whose motive was further networking in Washington and Hollywood. Celebrity journalism, as Tina practiced it, did not come cheap.

Out of boredom, or bubbling-over ambition, or perhaps sensing that she had gone as far as she could on Si Newhouse's money, in 1998 Tina Brown departed *The New Yorker* to begin a new magazine. Called *Talk,* which is how most gossip begins, it had the backing of Harvey Weinstein, head of Miramax, the movie studio. This time out, Tina would be creating something entirely her own, not building upon or resuscitating the work of precursors. Relying on roughly the same formula—that of gossip about the rich and famous—the plan was to make *Talk* sexy, racy, buzzy, and more insiderly than Napoleon's duodenum.

Talk never came off. Part of the problem may have been the reader, whom Tina imagined as "a woman in her thirties who wears Prada, watches Miramax movies, and uses Urbanfetch to order a Harry Potter book"—in other words, a woman who sounds a lot like Tina Brown. Part of the problem was staffing, getting the right editors and writers to fulfill her fantasy of a hot magazine. Moreover, the connection with Miramax was supposed to result in lots of pieces in *Talk* being used as fodder for Miramax movies. Didn't, as they say, happen.

Celebrity journalism is not usually directly deflationary or iconoclastic, but *Talk* was to have a strong touch of this to give it kick. A young editor at the magazine called one day to tell me that a department on reputations was planned, and Tina would love it if I were to take down some overrated figure in American life. I suggested Arthur Miller. "He's a terrible writer and even less impressive as a guru or a political saint," I said. The young editor thought it a swell idea, and said he would get back to me after he had run it by Tina. The next day he called to say that an Arthur Miller piece didn't feel quite right to Tina, but did I have any other ideas. "How about Walter Cronkite," I said, "a man with a face only a nation could love, and a genuinely unintelligent man, though the confident cadences of his broadcaster's fluency served to camouflage this over a long and hugely successful career." Great idea, the young editor said. The next day he called to say that Walter Cronkite didn't seem quite right to Tina, either.

Although she may have judged such subjects less than buzzy, my reading of these decisions was that Tina Brown thought these men too important to attack, whatever stir it might have caused. She was in fact only half an iconoclast, the other half a woman still on the way up and still in need of the aid of important people to get to higher places. We finally settled, the young editor, Tina Brown, and I, on the pompous literary critic Harold Bloom. I wrote the article, it was accepted and paid for ($5,000), but it never ran because *Talk* went out of business soon after I completed it.

The many people whose enmity Tina Brown earned were

pleased at her failure with *Talk.* They bruited it about that the main reason for the flop was that Tina had lost whatever magic she had in reading her old friend the Zeitgeist, that she was now herself out of all the important loops, and no longer a player, a contender for the kind of buzzy attention she was so expert at creating. Hillary Clinton, whom Tina supposedly admired, once remarked that "Tina is the junk food of journalism."

If Tina Brown may not truly be the lovable, huggable Miss Brown, she is surely, to cite not a song but a full musical, the Unsinkable Tina Brown. In 2003, a year after the collapse of *Talk,* she began a less than successful talk show on cable television, which lasted two years. She wrote a book on the poor dead airhead Princess Diana, filled with gossipy anecdotes.

As some women are good at finding husbands, Tina Brown has always been good at finding backers. Before long, with the financial support of Barry Diller, the movie and media man, she began the *Daily Beast,* a website known in the business as a news aggregator; she took stories from other newspapers and magazines and television stations, copied videos from talk and interview shows and YouTube, and hired a small staff of writers with a nose for gossip and controversy to contribute other items on subjects she thought hot or amusing. "I want this to be a speedy read that captures the Zeitgeist," she said. "We'll be smart and opinionated, looking to help cut through the volume [of news and information] with a keen sensibility. We're aiming for a curious, upscale and global audience who love politics, news and the media world."

The *Daily Beast* is Tina Brown's attempt to become the Mme. Récamier of the Twitter age. The website offers, she says, "a guided sensibility, with attitude." It's a site "that's really about tapping into the Zeitgeist"; it is "to move where the Zeitgeist is." As for its politics, it is to be "polypartisan," which means that it will attempt to be outside party politics: not disinterested, necessarily, but chiefly interested in the stories that best allow for insiderliness: the scandals, the defeats, just about anything, in other words, that can be personalized. "My bias is," Tina said, "is it interesting, is it provocative, is it amusing . . . does it go against received wisdom."

She clearly hopes that the *Daily Beast* will at last be the white ass upon which she will ride into Jerusalem. It's possible. But there are many competitors floating out there in cyberspace: the *Huffington Post,* the *Atlantic Wire,* and many more. Still, with her bounteous energy, as she approaches sixty, she's not a woman to be counted out.

She demonstrated that yet again when, toward the end of 2010, she helped engineer a partnership between the *Daily Beast* and the all but defunct *Newsweek,* which had been bought for its debt by a ninety-two-year-old audio manufacturer named Sidney Harman. "It means that the *Daily Beast's* animal high spirits will now be teamed with a legendary weekly print magazine in a joint venture, named The Newsweek Daily Beast Company," Tina announced in the *Daily Beast.* "As for me, I shall now be in the editor-in-chief's chair at both the *Daily Beast* and *Newsweek.*" Call her indefatigable, call her undefeatable, with her energy for hype, her robust false enthusiasm for the nonexistent (*Newsweek* "legendary"?), her really quite charming ability to pump up sugar daddies and exaggerate possibilities, Tina Brown, like her or not, is a phenomenon unto herself.

"We are living," she has said, "in an age where everyone wants to know everything about you." Her great skill has been to encourage a fundamental unseriousness in her readers. The serious after all requires thoughtful effort, even some brooding on subjects; on occasion it forces one to take painful, usually moral positions; and sometimes, yes, it can be quite boring. Tina Brown peddles entertainment, which is not against the law, but ought to be recognized for what it is: distraction. Master at psyching out the Zeitgeist, she has become very much part of that same Zeitgeist, the purest type we have of the contemporary journalist, a woman whose goal, though she may not know it, is the excruciatingly boring state where everything is merely interesting and nothing finally is important.

Diary

She adored his writing, absolutely worshiped it. So when he was to give a reading at her university, she was the first to show up at the auditorium where he was to appear. She was standing in the back of the room when he approached her.

"Excuse me," he said in his greenhorn's English, "are you here for the reading?"

"I am," she said. "You're Mr. Singer, aren't you? I can't tell you how much I admire your writing. You are the only author today whose work will be read a hundred years from now. I am so honored to meet you."

"Thank you," he said. "But tell me, are you Jewish?"

"I am," she said.

"And where, if I may ask, is your family from in Europe?"

"Bialystok," she said, "on both my parents' sides."

"Oh," he said, "I know a great deal about Bialystok. Maybe we might meet after the reading and you can tell me what you know about your family's history in that fascinating city."

"That would be very nice," she said.

He was completely charming at his reading, for which the auditorium was filled. And he was even more so during the question-and-answer session. Someone asked him if he believed in free will. "Of course I believe in free will," he replied. "What choice have I?"

She went to the reception after the reading, where, after forty or so minutes, he disengaged himself from his admirers and came up to her.

"If you'd like to tell me what you know about your family's history in the city of Bialystok, I have some rooms in this building. We could do it now."

She followed him to the small apartment the university provided him: a sitting room with a couch, two chairs, a round table with a bowl of fruit on it, and a bedroom behind a closed door.

She sat on one end of the couch, he at the other end. He was small and hairless—did he suffer from alopecia? she wondered—but with the coloring of a former redhead. He was wearing a shirt with small green polka dots and a black knit tie with a thick knot.

"So, *nu*, tell me what you know about Bialystok."

She began to rattle off the few facts in her possession, and hadn't got more than three minutes into it when he made his move.

"Excuse me," he said, leaning slightly forward. "May I kiss you?"

Good God, she thought, how naïve she was to let herself get into this situation. She recalled how sexy so many of his stories and novels are. Such realistic descriptions didn't come from nowhere. But the thought of being in bed with this man, who was at least thirty years older than she, and who reminded her of no one so much as her grandfather, was, beyond chilling, unthinkable.

"Oh, Mr. Singer," she said, "I am honored, please believe me, but I have to tell you that I have only recently begun my second marriage, and I don't really—"

He put up his hand, signaling her to cease all further explanations.

"No, no, no," he said with a smile. "Don't worry. Here"— he pointed to the bowl on the table—"take some fruit to your husband."

She got up from the couch, went over to the bowl, and picked out an immense Delicious apple and a green banana. When she looked back toward the couch, he was gone.

18

Too Much Even of Kreplach

I never repeat gossip, so listen carefully.
— LIZ SMITH

ALL RELIGIONS CLAIM to abhor gossip, but Judaism, to my knowledge, is the only religion to have codified its abhorrence. *Lashon hara,* or evil tongue, is a high-ranking Jewish sin about which a great deal has been written. A book, *Chafetz Chaim (Seeker of Life),* by Rabbi Yisrael Meir Kagan, is devoted entirely to guiding the reader on correct speech and the avoidance of slander. The subject is one that brings out all that is best, and worst, in the Talmudic mind, a mind that, capable of astonishing feats of memory and intellectual penetration, can sometimes also exult in the finest of hairsplitting.

The Talmudists take passages from Psalms ("Keep your tongue from evil and your lips from speaking guile," 34:13), from Exodus ("You shall not utter a false report," 23:1, and "From a false matter you shall distance yourself," 23:7), and two from Leviticus ("In righteousness shall you judge your kinsman," 19:15, and "Do not go about as a tale bearer among your people," 19:16), and run with them, really take off. Lots of supporting scripture is sometimes brought to bear in the argument against *lashon hara.* As many as 31 of the 613 *mitzvot,* or rules and principles of law and ethics, set out in Jewish law, are shown to be violated through the act of gossip. The main drift of the argument is clear enough: it is sinful to initiate gossip and quite as sinful to repeat it, and it is even a sin to listen to it.

Reading rabbinic instruction on the spiritual dangers of *lashon hara* and on the complexity entailed in avoiding it, one recognizes afresh the high degree of virtue required of anyone who can completely omit the evident, one is inclined to say natural, pleasure that gossip gives. "Mrs. [Isabella Stewart] Gardner," George Santayana wrote in *Persons and Places* of the great Boston art patron, "though she defied prudery, practiced the virtue most difficult for a brilliant woman in a hostile society: she spoke ill of no one." Not many Mrs. Gardners around in our day.

Coming away from reading about gossip in the Talmud, one recognizes how much a part of human nature gossip seems. But then the role of religion has never been to accept raw human nature as a completed enterprise, but to attempt to tame, alter, hone, and refine the coarseness of human nature into something grander than it is. Religion may take credit for much in the way of civilizing human beings, but in the realm of gossip it hasn't, I think it fair to say, made much headway.

"I really believe," says Bonnie Fuller, who has edited *Cosmopolitan, Glamour, US Weekly,* and other gossipy magazines, "we all have a gossip gene." Bonnie Fuller is no geneticist, but is in fact a gossip professional who currently runs Hollywoodlife.com, a celebrity website, and when the word "celebrity" is used as an adjective, the safe assumption is that gossip is what it is about. But whether we have something resembling a gossip gene or not, anyone who has a wide curiosity, or merely wishes to understand the world, or wishes merely to carry on with normal social life, has from time to time to listen to gossip, and after listening to it will feel the need to contribute a squib or two of it on his or her own. Gossip, perhaps almost as much as money, makes the social world go round.

I was not long ago talking baseball with a friend, and lamenting, as Chicagoans are wont to do, the wretchedness of the Cubs.

I brought up the team's many foolish trades of players who went on to become superstars on other teams. One of the worst of such trades was getting rid of the slugger Rafael Palmeiro, who—with the aid of steroids, to be sure—went on to hit more than five hundred home runs for the Texas Rangers and Baltimore Orioles. "Here they really had no choice," my friend said. "Palmeiro was having a fling with X's"—and here he mentioned the team's most popular player, who later got into the Hall of Fame—"first wife, and this was obviously a potential disaster, so the front office decided to get rid of Palmeiro and keep X. No other way they could go."

Is this true? Who knows? But it is a fascinating speculation, and a fascinating speculation will almost always trump a dull explanation. "Fascinating speculation"—in that phrase we have yet another definition of gossip, one that accounts for at least half of all gossip. Like most surgery, gossip is by its nature invasive. As such, it seeks to penetrate the social skin we all wear as protection over our truer self in order to probe beneath to those psychologically tender places—pride, shame, fear of humiliation, insecurity, and the rest—that are likely, the hope of gossip is, to reveal that truer, less impressive, more genuine self. The social theorist Erving Goffman wrote a book called *The Presentation of Self in Everyday Life* in which he distinguished between the before-the-footlights, or public, self presented to the world, and the backstage, or private, self where we appear without makeup, hair down, in deshabille. Gossip seeks to reveal this inner, no doubt vain, fantasy-producing, pathetic, less than lovely self, and do with it what it wishes. And what it wishes is generally not benign.

Oppressive societies—Communist Russia and China, Nazi Germany, the Taliban, and others—have made strenuous efforts to block gossip, which can also be subversive. I don't know if anyone has ever written about it—it would be a complicated subject to document—but it is difficult to imagine a revolution from below taking place without the aid of roiling gossip. This would be the kind stirred by resentment and envy—look how our leaders, our clergy, our capitalists, live, the pigs!—featuring the decadence of the ruling class and the mistreatment of the underclass. Marie-Antoinette and her husband, Louis XVI, met the guillotine owing to such gossip. Gossip can be a powerful igniter of revolutions.

In times of anxiety or actual crisis, rumors naturally crop up with greater frequency, and gossip spreads commensurately to keep up with them. Stirring the muddy waters, gossip at such times is likely to be even more emphatic, hyperbolic, high-flying, and far-fetched, more distorted and distorting than old-fashioned backyard-fence gossip or artful Oxbridge common room or witty gay gossip. Some eras are more gossip-ridden than others. Different economic systems produce different kinds of gossip: socialist gossip tends to be about envy ("She has so much more than we do"), capitalist gossip about greed ("You'll be shocked when I tell you how much she inherited"). In Karl Marx's daydreams, once the dictatorship of the proletariat had come to power, such would be universal happiness, all gossip, like private ownership, would have been eliminated. Hasn't happened yet.

What might gossip's vast, oil-spill-like spread, in America and elsewhere, mean? One possibility is a dumbing down of cultural and intellectual life. We all suffer intellectual impatience, and it may be that the country itself, after decades of television watching, photo ops, quotable quotes, and the rest, has a much-reduced attention span. Gossip, after all, doesn't call for much in the way of attention or patience. Quite the reverse: its penchant is for the bottom line, going for the groin—who is sleeping with whom, who is stealing and how much, who is hiding the most bestial private behavior. Gossip serves it up straight; leave your subtlety or taste for complex reality at the door.

Economic arrangements in the United States have added to the strong flow of gossip by supplying many more people to gossip about. By "economic arrangements" I mean the numbers of people in certain professions—entertainment, sports, some of the arts, the financial world—making enormous amounts of money. The very rich acquire celebrity stature through the brute fact of their wealth. (The world awaits degrading stories about Bill Gates and Warren Buffett.) Fortunes create celebrity, and celebrities, playing the game skillfully with the aid of money managers, usually acquire fortunes. The number of celebrities has been growing for a long while. As far back as the 1920s, Virginia Woolf remarked, "This celebrity business is quite chronic." She would be appalled at how much more critical things in this regard are today.

Those of us bereft of vast fortunes or celebrity tend to be interested in those who have either, or sometimes both, in amplitude. Our interest is responsible for creating the extensive cadre of gossip professionals, men and women who make their living off this interest. The most canny among them realize that behind that interest runs the strong green thread of envy; and they know, too, that no form of gossip has wider appeal than that about the rich and famous, the naturally talented and beautiful, who have fallen on bad times. Schadenfreude, the pleasure taken from the misfortune of others, is one off which gossips, professional and amateur, have ever fed.

Good taste was once a partial prophylactic against gossip, but now less and less so. The triumph of therapy, in all its many branches and divisions, long ago snuffed out much good taste in the name of candor and health through confession. Under the reign of a therapy triumphant, inhibition has no place, repression is the enemy. Don't hold back, Jack; let it spill, Jill—such are the dominant if unspoken encouragements of therapy. No secrets permitted among friends; even one's friend's secrets bestowed upon one in confidence don't hold the weight they once did. This marks an enormous change in the etiquette of social life in our country, and a great boost for gossip.

"I hate gossip," proclaimed the philosopher A. J. Ayer, "but I do love truth." Ayer, you should know, was an ardent gossip, and used to meet with the philosopher Gilbert Ryle, the historian Hugh Trevor-Roper, and the classicist Maurice Bowra in lengthy sessions in one another's rooms at Oxford, in which, with artful malice reinforced by the gift of wild comic formulation, they tore apart colleagues, enemies and ostensible friends both.

Ayer's formulation—hate gossip, love truth—points up the epistemological problem about gossip, namely: What is its truth content, and how much can it be trusted? Here we come to both the fascination and the discouragement of gossip. For gossip is rich stories, tantalizing, sometimes titillating, often tremendously amusing, but in the end, because usually unascertainable, less than fully satisfying. Like astrology, psychoanalysis, and other pseudoscientific endeavors, gossip promises to provide significant secrets. Sometimes it does, but often it comes up empty.

Fascinating though gossip can be, to retain its charm it needs to be taken in modest portions. "You can have too much," as the novelist Isaac Bashevis Singer used to say, "even of kreplach," the Jewish delicacy that is a meat dumpling served in chicken soup. And with gossip we seem currently to have arrived at the too much stage and perhaps gone beyond it. Yet the appetite for gossip shows no signs of slackening.

Gossip may well have spread in the way it has because so few among us are any longer trained in the skill of ascertaining truthful statements. Or have most of us lost our belief in truth itself; found that truth is simply unavailable in contemporary journalism, print or electronic; think truth no longer a precise but a proximate, relative thing, and so, as in the game of horseshoes, close to the truth is good enough? Because of this we are more and more at home with what Matt Drudge calls "unedited information," of the kind one finds floating in the ether of the Internet, the appetite for which, as Drudge contends (and who is to say he is wrong?), grows greater and greater.

Once a secret vice, gossip threatens to become the chief way we obtain our information, and there doesn't appear to be much anyone can do about it. All very well to call gossip a moral blight, which in many ways it is. Yet it seems to come so naturally to most of us, who take such unalloyed delight in it. Who is to stop its torrential flow? The likelihood of getting people, through religious prohibition or moral suasion, to stop contributing to the immense fund of current gossip, or to cease enjoying such lively gossip as comes their way, is what mathematicians call a negative integer, or something less than zero. Gossip is here to stay, and figures to increase. "Live with it," as the kids say, and we may as well learn to do so, because living without the intrusions of gossip seems unlikely except in a Trappist monastery, and maybe, gossip has it, not even there.

A Bibliographical Note

If there is a single book on the subject of gossip with the ample pretensions to the one you have just read, I did not find it. As for those pretensions, they include the attempt to report for a general, intelligent reader on what gossip is, how it works, and how it has changed over the years. Instead there are many books — some academic, some popular, some plain vulgar — that set out to explore various aspects of gossip, or gossip in different realms of life: politics, show business, literary life.

I have leaned rather heavily on certain books for the biographical portions of my book: on the *Memoirs of the Duc de Saint-Simon* for my portrait of the Duc; on Neal Gabler's solid *Walter Winchell: Gossip, Power, and the Culture of Celebrity* for my portrait of Winchell; on Judy Bachrach's richly gossipy *Tina and Harry Come to America* for my portrait of Tina Brown; and on Barbara Walters's autobiography, *Audition*, for my portrait of her.

I do not list here the number of novels I read and found useful for my study of gossip, except those I specifically talk about in the pages of the book. Next to life itself, superior novels are the richest source of observation of the glory and antics of human beings we have. Novels have been at the center of my education, and remain there. When the Oxford philosopher Gilbert Ryle was asked if he read novels, he replied, "Yes, all six," by which he meant he read only the novels of Jane Austen, implying one needn't read many others. My own novel-reading habits are not so chaste, and there has rarely been a time in my adult life when I didn't have a bookmark in a novel in progress. And few of the novels I have read have not, in one form or another, pivoted on, played off, or otherwise made use of gossip.

Memoirs, diaries, and letters of famous and sometimes secondary people have been another rich source in the making of this book. Such forms are, by their nature, open invitations to indiscretion, which is to say, gossip-filled—and if they aren't, they are unlikely to be of great interest.

Gossip in print is almost as bountiful as gossip in conversation, and here is a list of the works—some immensely gossipy, some attempting to explain gossip—that I have drawn on for my own book:

Austen, Jane, *Persuasion*

Bachrach, Judy, *Tina and Harry Come to America*

Bergmann, Jörg, *Discreet Indiscretions: The Social Organization of Gossip*

Bok, Sissela, *Secrets: On the Ethics of Concealment and Revelation*

Braudy, Leo, *The Frenzy of Renown: Fame and Its History*

Brown, Tina, *The Diana Chronicles*

Capote, Truman, *Too Brief a Treat: The Letters of Truman Capote*, edited by Gerald Clarke

Collins, Gail, *Scorpion Tongues: The Irresistible History of Gossip in American Politics*

Coward, Noël, *The Diaries of Noël Coward*, edited by Graham Payn and Sheridan Moreley

Coward, Noël, *The Letters of Noël Coward*, edited and with commentary by Barry Day

Eliot, George, *Daniel Deronda*

Gabler, Neal, *Walter Winchell: Gossip, Power, and the Culture of Celebrity*

Goodman, Robert F., and Aaron Ben-Ze'ev, editors, *Good Gossip*

James, Henry, *The Reverberator*

Lerman, Leo, *The Grand Surprise: The Journals of Leo Lerman*, edited by Stephen Pascal

McKelway, St. Clair, *Gossip: The Life and Times of Walter Winchell*

Pym, Barbara, *Crampton Hodnet*

Rader, Dotson, *Tennessee: Cry from the Heart*

Raphael, Frederic, *Byron*

Schickel, Richard, *Intimate Strangers: The Culture of Celebrity in America*

Solove, Daniel J., *The Future of Reputation: Gossip, Rumor, and Privacy on the Internet*

Spacks, Patricia Meyer, *Gossip*

Sterling, Barbara, *Secrets of a Tabloid Reporter: My Twenty Years on the* National Enquirer*'s Hollywood Beat*

Suetonius, *The Twelve Caesars*

Sunstein, Cass, *On Rumors: How Falsehoods Spread, Why We Believe Them, What Can Be Done*

Trevor-Roper, Hugh, *Letters from Oxford: Hugh Trevor-Roper to Bernard Berenson,* edited by Richard Davenport Hines

Tynan, Kenneth, *Diaries of Kenneth Tynan,* edited by John Lahr

Walls, Jeannette, *Dish: How Gossip Became the News, and the News Became Just Another Show*

Walters, Barbara, *Audition*

White, Edmund, *City Boy*

Wilkes, Roger, *Scandal: A Scurrilous History*

Williams, Tennessee, *Memoirs*

Index